Gerald Dawe was born in Belfast in 1952 and educated at Orangefield Boys' School in the city, University of Ulster and National University of Ireland, Galway. He has published six collections of poetry, including *Sunday School* (1991), *The Morning Train* (1999) and *Lake Geneva* (2003). He has also published *The Proper Word: Collected Criticism* (2007). A fellow of Trinity College, Dublin, Gerald Dawe lives in Dun Laoghaire, County Dublin.

By the same author

Poetry
Sheltering Places
The Lundys Letter
Sunday School
Heart of Hearts
The Morning Train
Lake Geneva

Criticism
How's the Poetry Going?
A Real Life Elsewhere
False Faces
Against Piety
The Rest is History
Stray Dogs and Dark Horses
The Proper Word: Collected Criticism
(ed. Nicholas Allen)

MY MOTHER-CITY

MY MOTHER-CITY

GERALD DAWE

LAGAN PRESS
BELFAST
2007

Acknowledgements

'My Mother-City' is an updated and expanded version of 'The Burning Ground' section from a chapbook originally published in 1998 by The Abbey Press and entitled *The Rest is History*. Some sections of 'Bit Parts' also appeared there. Kind acknowledgement is made to Adrian Rice and Mel McMahon who worked on that edition. Thanks are also due to those friends and colleagues who encouraged me in the early days, and I particularly want to thank Van Morrison and Rev. Gary Hastings, both of whom gave of their time and knowledge. Lyrics by Van Morrison are quoted with the permission of Exile Productions. Additional excerpts of this book appeared in 'Revenges of the Heart', *The Cities of Belfast*, edited by Nicholas Allen and Aaron Kelly (Dublin: Four Courts Press, 2003), *Agenda*, *Fortnight*, the *Irish News*, the Ulster Society publications and broadcast on BBC Northern Ireland and RTE. Poems by Gerald Dawe are published by the Gallery Press (www.gallerypress.com).

The author kindly acknowledges the assistance of the School of English, Trinity College, Dublin, An Chomhairle Ealaíon/The Arts Council, Ireland, Cultural Relations Committee, Department of Sport, Tourism and the Arts, The Department of Foreign Affairs, Dublin, The British Council, Ireland and Culture Ireland.

Published by
Lagan Press
1A Bryson Street
Belfast BT5 4ES
e-mail: lagan-press@e-books.org.uk
web: lagan-press.org.uk

© Gerald Dawe, 2007

The moral right of the author has been asserted.

ISBN (10 digit): 1 904652 42 5
ISBN (13 digit): 978 1 904652 42 7
Author: Dawe, Gerald
Title: My Mother-City
2007

Design: December
Printed by J.H. Haynes, Sparkford

for Iarla and Olwen

Contents

My Mother-City *13*

Bit Parts *109*

I

MY MOTHER-CITY

'This was my mother-city, these my paps.'
—Louis MacNeice

COMING INTO BELFAST IS LIKE APPROACHING a sunken city. It lies inside a horseshoe of surrounding hills; the coastal land to its southern shoreline is the rich, undulating landscape of County Down; to Belfast's northerly shores is County Antrim: a harsher, dramatic terrain that faces Scotland across the narrow straits of the sea of Moyle.

Unlike most Irish cities, which give their name to the immediate hinterland—Dublin, Galway, Cork, Sligo, Waterford, Derry, Donegal—Belfast is just itself. The lough at whose mouth the city fans out is fed by the river Lagan, which flows down through the untouched meadows and park forests, along embankments and under the bridges which link the south and east of the city with the north and west.

In the building docks and islands, old quays and wharves, Belfast's industrial history as a shipbuilding and merchant port makes way for the new transport of ferry terminals. The channels such as Victoria and Musgrave and basins like Pollock, which had borne tankers, liners and gunships for the British fleet, rub shoulders now with a busy and expanding City airport. The massive gantries of the Harland & Wolff shipbuilders—once the greatest of their kind in the world—straddle the city's horizon like monumental arches.

Clutched around Belfast's inner reaches, the refitted mills and factories, warehouses and engineering works, are isolated by the svelte dominance of motorway and bypass.

What remains of Belfast's industrial architecture has a strange marooned look to it. Similarly, the red-brick Gothic of insurance houses and banks, stores and churches, hotels and theatres, which was once the city's Victorian legacy, has all but vanished. Belfast underwent the fate of many cities in Britain and Ireland caught and mauled by the hectic redevelopment boom of the 1980s. What have taken over, inside out as it were, are the shopping mall, the steel-framed Centre and the masked facade. These changes belie another truth, however: of the profound, irrevocable change Belfast experienced as the site of sectarian violence which took possession of the city from the late 1960s: bombing campaigns in the name of Irish national liberation vied with bombing campaigns in the name of preserving the British way of life. Peace-lines of metal girders divided communities against themselves; security barriers defaced the cityscape and turned the centre into a police zone during the worst years of the Troubles.

The map of the city is a history of territorial allegiances and tribal loyalties. To quote from Jonathan Bardon's definitive history, *Belfast: An Illustrated History*:

> Whether or not the citizens of Belfast regularly practised their religion, the vast majority unhesitatingly felt themselves either to be Protestant or Catholic. It was amongst the working-classes that segregation was most complete, especially in Ballymacarrett and the Falls-Shankill region of west Belfast.

For anyone growing up in the Belfast of the late 1940s and 50s there was always going to be an inbred sense of where one literally walked. This sense of place has been grotesquely theatricalised as a result of the Troubles and the physical institutionalisation of sectarian divisions during the 1970s and 80s. But it is true to say that over the generations, Belfast people, particularly working-class people, were born with second sight; a radar as to where one was in the city. Lacking such instinct could spell danger in the night life of Belfast and most certainly led to many a harsh word and 'scrap' (or street-fight). Eventually, the political divisions of the city, crackling like an electric storm in the future, were earthed in precisely these intensely intimate and cross-grained inner lives of the city's myriad neighbourhoods.

In the late 60s and early 1970s, what had once been a 'mixed' neighbourhood where Protestant and Catholic families had 'got on well', experienced the shock of having to face the truth about Belfast's sectarian divisions. Similarly, the traditional Protestant and traditional Catholic areas which had previously been negotiable by bus or foot, when leaving a girl home after a dance, or meeting a pal, or going to a party, became increasingly more dangerous and ultimately amounted to a perilous risk upon which few would chance their lives. By the mid-1970s when assassination squads roamed what became known as 'twilight zones', or interfaces between the dominant working-class districts, Belfast had ceased to be a living city and had become, for a decade and more, a ghost town.

Districts played, and still play, a key role in defining the identity of Belfast. Even though there have been extraordinary population shifts within the city over the last twenty-five years, because of intimidation and violence, on the one hand, and redevelopment on the other, the sense of being *from* a particular area is strong and lasting. It is a pattern common to many industrial cities such as Belfast.

Put at its simplest, Belfast's history is physically indistinguishable from the industries, which were established, in the nineteenth and twentieth centuries: linen-mills, ropeworks, tobacco factories, shipbuilding, engineering works.

Erected literally within this formidable industrial landscape were the streets and houses of the workers. It is not physically possible to think about Belfast as if it were different from this industrial past. Consequently, Belfast is unique in Ireland and has much more in common with Liverpool or Glasgow since the pattern of its streets, as much as the commercial nature of the city, centred on the industrial heartland; little else.

Each district had its own factories; its own customs linked to the work-practices of the factory; its own destiny, and well-being, tied irrevocably to that factory. The Falls, a predominantly Catholic road, had its mills; York Street in the Protestant lower north side had the famous Gallaher's tobacco factory while the shipyards dominated the east of the city. It was a pattern replicated throughout the city, layer by layer, from the dockland upwards until the prosperous higher roads circle the outer city, heading for the nearby countryside.

This pattern rapidly disappeared in the post-industrial 1990s. By the early years of the new millennium developments along the Lagan waterfront transformed parts of the city into apartment villages and multinational 'nowheres'. Going back forty years, it was a fact of life that those who grew up in the districts surrounding, or, more like, hugging the industrial shore, would become part of it. The stories of their lives were the story of the industries in which they worked. Indeed, one reason for the fierceness of the sectarian passion, which has characterised Belfast throughout much of its history, is the struggle to maintain some standard of living in a city whose economy was (and, of course, remains) fundamentally susceptible to the unpredictable diktats of the UK government in Westminster.

What were known were the streets where one lived; they were predictable. Families stayed, generation through generation, and while the men in the house (and sometimes the daughters) might follow work 'across the water' (to Britain) or emigrate further afield to Canada or Australia, the home territory was a proven ground.

Here the rituals of Belfast life were handed down via the calendar of quasi-religious rites and political commemorations.

For the Protestant community, in the main identifying themselves with the union with Britain, their sense of being different from the Irish nationalist cultural and political aspirations of the Catholic community was celebrated in the past through Orange parades and marches. Taking place annually throughout the summer months of July and August, these parades in Belfast were dramatised statements of territorial imperatives and cultural bonding. If Cork or Limerick had Corpus Christi,

Belfast, or those parts, which called themselves Protestant, had the Twelfth.

The serried ranks of bedecked men, in good suits and bowler hats, with sashes and silver insignias pinned onto armlets and lapels, wearing immaculate white gloves and carrying huge silken banners that swayed like canopies in the wind, were an amazing and quite disturbing sight. Carrying the symbols of the British Crown and Imperial past as if they were religious relics, these men assembled in the back streets to demonstrate their loyalty to Queen and Faith and Country.

The major roads and avenues into the centre of the town and beyond the city to a field of worship were transformed into a bizarre occasion caught somewhere between the mood of Mardi Gras and the formal opening of a Guild Hall. Meanwhile behind such a contradictory carnival—which included the pagan-like burning of bonfires on the Eleventh Night, the night before the marching took place, and the sombre declaration of Protestant religious beliefs—the Catholic community either left the city if they could afford to, kept in doors or observed from a safe distance these men and their followers as they sang and danced through large parts of the city, and the city's centre.

Again, much has changed over the years (the Twelfth is being re-branded Orangefest, for a start!) and the power of the Twelfth Marches of the Orange Order has dwindled into an exotic and effectively symbolic reminder of the divisions, which have underscored the city's history and its contested territories, street by street.

From such loci, however, the co-ordinates of life in Belfast were formed. Antennae of curiosity could identify invisible barriers, marking out the social parameters within which people lived. To know where someone lived was tantamount to knowing his or her religion. Received wisdom could then take over.

Moving out from where the City Hall sits inside Donegall Square, the roads and avenues form a compass of religious and cultural division. Rising up out of Donegall Place, Royal Avenue and York Street are the famous districts of the Falls, Shankill and Crumlin: what is now called West Belfast. Turning east towards the Lagan and crossing the river 'over the bridge' are the Newtownards, Albertbridge, Beersbridge and Woodstock districts. The land is densely housed, each neighbourhood a protectorate all on its own.

The predominantly Protestant east of the city is like a triangular wedge, bordered by one of the longest roads in the city—the Newtownards Road—and by the Castlereagh and Knock roads. Within the triangle reside the neighbourhoods of Ballymacarrett, Bloomfield, Strandtown, Ballyhackamore, Castlereagh, Cregagh and Orangefield.

The streetscapes are familiar to anyone who has lived in a provincial industrial city. East Belfast in particular was defined by that industrial past since shipbuilding physically dominated the horizon. In a literal and imaginative sense the gantries, sirens, workers' houses and buses; the very sounds and sights of post-war Belfast were determined by the ups and downs of the shipbuilding orders at the two great industrial sites of Harland and Wolff and Workman and Clark. 'By 1959', remarks Jonathan Bardon, 'the works covered 300 acres'. Indeed, it may be difficult to appreciate today the extent to which Belfast had once been a leading industrial presence throughout the world. At least three of its industries—shipbuilding, ropeworks and linen—were the largest of their kind at one time or another. Leslie

Clarkson looks back to the early years of the twentieth century and sees Belfast's dominance not simply in Irish terms:

> There were a few small shipbuilding and repairing yards in Dublin, Londonderry and elsewhere, but their importance was declining and their output negligible. Belfast's importance was, in fact, greater than simple percentages indicate, for her yards concentrated on big ships for the merchant marine and Royal Navy, not small tramp and coastal steamers. It was around the Belfast shipbuilding industry, and to a lesser extent the textile industry, that the engineering industry clustered. Except for steam-engine manufacture, agricultural machinery, railway engineering and cycle making, Belfast was dominant in all branches of engineering in Ireland, and its textile machinery, in particular, had worldwide renown.

Queen's Island, the symbolic heartland of east Belfast, was the site of the leading shipbuilding business in the world throughout the 1950s. Terence Brown, the cultural historian and literary critic, has accurately defined the parameters of this industrial world in, 'Let's Go to Graceland', a memoir of the east Belfast-born playwright, Stewart Parker:

> On any working morning men poured over the bridge that spanned the Lagan and out of the narrow streets of red brick kitchen houses into the shipyard that still saw itself with the Clyde [Glasgow] as a world power in that heroic industry. The rope works were the largest in the world and you could believe it watching the shawlies [women factory workers] teeming around its gates as the hooter sounded summoning them to work through the foggy murk of a part of the city

that seemed always in semi-darkness. And there was the aircraft factory and aerodrome too.

Shipbuilding, ropeworks, aircraft, linen mills, manufacturing of one kind or another; the allied business of commercial and corporation administration; central and local government; service industries—all had turned Belfast into a thriving industrial post-war city. Precious wonder that from John Keats' description in 1818 of 'passing into Belfast through a most wretched suburb' and hearing 'that most disgusting of all noises ... the sound of the [linen mill's] shuttle' to Louis MacNeice's poem 'Valediction', the image of Belfast was exclusively one of a city defined by work. MacNeice's 30s Belfast is 'devout and profane and hard':

> Built on reclaimed mud, hammers playing in the shipyard,
> Time punched with holes like a steel sheet, time
> Hardening the faces, veneering with a grey
>   and speckled rime
> The faces under the shawls and caps:
> This was my mother-city, these my paps.

MacNeice was to change his mind and discover beneath the seemingly unchangeable 'outer ugliness and dourness' a deeper reality which he found upon his regular visits back to the city during the 1950s. But the simple truth of the matter is that modern Belfast was a city founded upon heavy industry, and east Belfast developed out of that cauldron. Such historical reality cannot tell the whole story, nevertheless.

Around the (now defunct) rope and engineering works, streets of parlour and kitchen houses ('two-up-two-downs') give unto wider roads and avenues, wealthy parks and gardens before becoming the countryside.

This is how Brenda Collins traces the established pattern of housing and civic and visual amenity in the early decades of the twentieth century as Belfast's population rapidly increased:

> Its roots were in the early industrial development of the city and the subsequent exodus of the middle and professional classes from their Donegall Square townhouses, whose grandeur had declined as the smoky industrial chimneys increased, to the more spacious and airy suburbs. Doctors and financiers, solicitors and architects now separated their home lives from their professional lives. This movement was most obvious in the south of the city where the middle class suburbs of the Malone ridge and the University area were a much more healthy environment than lower down Dublin Road near the 'nuisance' of the River Blackstaff, which was contaminated by the refuse of mills and factories ... To the north of the city centre overlooking the shores of Belfast Lough, the former deerpark of the Donegalls was divided into Oldpark and Newpark. Northwards from Carlisle Circus areas such as Mount Vernon, Parkmount and Duncairn and the loughside estates of the Grove, Fortwilliam and Skegoniel grew from the parcelling out of villa parkland into attractive sites for the aspiring lower middle class of commercial clerks and manufacturers' agents ... Across the Lagan, beyond industrial Ballymacarett and Lagan village, a vigorous suburban development was also under way, and the estates of Ormeau, Ravenhill, Rosetta, Annadale, Knock, Belmont and Stormont were gradually replaced by neat avenues and parades of new villas.

The significance of these distinctions should not be lost to us. Belfast clearly was, and still is, a civic landscape of class distinction. 'The pattern', writes political historian Patrick Buckland, 'was established well before partition but became more pronounced afterwards as a result of intimidation in "times" of crisis and the pressure of local politics'. Buckland goes on:

> In the former instance, families of the 'wrong sort' were driven out of their homes or considered it advisable to leave, while local politicians were concerned to maintain if not enlarge their majorities by the careful allocation of houses among electoral areas. Segregation was most marked in Belfast. The Falls became almost exclusively Catholic, as Catholics of all social groups moved into the area, which in the nineteenth century had been a working class preserve. As a necessary corollary, the main Protestant districts became even more homogeneous, although without the same admixture of classes.

The final clause in Patrick Buckland's last sentence is particularly revealing here. While 'Protestant districts', such as East Belfast were 'even more homogeneous' in terms of religious affiliation than their Catholic counterpoints in other parts of the city, there was not 'the same admixture of classes'. What in effect Buckland is alluding to is the important housing differences as working-class housing bordered upon lower-middle-class housing which in turn bordered upon middle-class housing and so on. In other words, a class-conscious, incremental, tier-system.

Streetscapes altered, widened and opened out the further one moved up and away from the city basin and its immediate hinterland. From a very early age, Belfast children learned their place in this scheme of things; it was part of their physical surroundings, assimilating architectural and civic barriers of class as much as absorbing, and sometimes, rejecting, or transcending as best

Eason and Sons, Great Victoria Street Railway Station, 1956.

they could, the discreet signs of religious—and hence, political identity.

Accents, too, played a specific, instructive role in deciding within seconds one's background. For working-class kids who lived in what would approximate today to 'the inner city', the 'posh areas' were merely a step away, in one sense, and, in another, a whole world away. To know one's own place was not only a source of strength but also an inhibition. It was often out on weekend walks through these avenues and parks that one saw the different styles of life counterpoised quite starkly with one's own. Houses like mansions; tree-lined driveways; gardens like parks. Sedate, discreet, private. A landscape of imaginative thresholds amounted to a metaphor of the imagination itself. Yet within the intimate, even claustrophobic closeness of the working-class districts there were the random open spaces of builders' yards, fugitive rivers and streams, old warehouses, industrial networks and vast walls. And echoes, if one but knew, of the city's Gaelic palimpsest, charted with such care by Patrick McKay in his essay 'Belfast Placenames and the Irish Language'.

For a young boy or girl, part of 'a gang of mates', life growing up in such a district was like a pendulum-swing between adventure and boredom, dreaming and routine, desire crossing against the force of custom, expectation and convention.

Things were close at hand: local cinemas and shops, school and church, sport and clubs, bars and walks—all available within the community. The outside world, whether that be London or America, lived in the imagination, fed by film, or the radio, or magazines, or letters and parcels from an uncle or aunt; one of the displaced family. After the ravages of World War II, Belfast, like so many other cities which had experienced at first hand the reality of war—the Blitz of 1941 had left over 700 dead and whole areas of the city destroyed—was busy trying to come to terms with peace. But the city had been exposed, in a storm of outrage, blame and shame, to the fact that many of its citizens had been living in appalling housing conditions. Furthermore, the Blitz, having forced tens of thousands from the city, presented startling evidence of the evacuees' poor state of health. The late 1940s and 50s mark a time when practical solutions to some of these problems were attempted, particularly in the fields of housing, health and education. What did not change, however, were the basic religious and political demographic fault-lines of the city. Some voices forecasted trouble if these deep-seated and by now visible grievances of the ordinary people were not addressed. According to historian Jonathan Bardon, while 'the Second World War had been far more harrowing than the First', for the citizens of Belfast, 'the sense of optimism and hope seemed stronger than in 1918; to a large extent this was justified'.

Born in 1945 in Belfast, as World War II ended and optimism and hope grew, the early years of Van Morrison follow a traditional pattern, at least on the surface. His surname in Ulster draws together the province's Gaelic roots. According to Robert Bell, Morrison is among 'the thirty most numerous names in Scotland' while its Irish origin as O'Muirgheasain (from Muirgheas meaning 'sea valour') is in County Donegal, the most westerly of the Ulster counties.

Indeed the exchange and cross-fertilisation between Ulster and Scotland are imbedded in the Morrison name itself.

As Robert Bell explains, a branch of the Donegal O'Morrisons migrated at some unknown date from Inishowen 'to Lewis and Harris in the Scottish Isles' where some 'became bards to the MacLeods'.

In *Scottish Clans and Tartans*, Ian Grimble elaborates upon the Morrisons as a clan of Scandinavian extraction, their founder being a natural son of the King of Norway, cast ashore on the Scottish island of Lewis.

> A legend tells that [the Morrisons] were first shipwrecked ... so that their clan badge is driftwood. Clan genealogies trace their descent from Somerled, the King of the Isles who died in 1164 and probably descended from the Celto-Norse King of Ireland ... One of the most memorable Morrisons of Lewis is Ruaraidth (or Roderick in its anglicised form) who was born there in about 1660. He is remembered as An Clarsail

Dall, the Blind Piper, and in fact he holds the highest place in the traditions of his country ... 'Oran Mor Mhic Leoid' [is] surely one of the most beautiful of Gaelic laments. In it he not only mourned the death of his patron at Dunvegan, but also the passing of the old Celtic culture there under his anglicised successor.

Other references to Morrison pick out the overlapping connections, historically and culturally, between Ulster and Scotland, and mythopoetically with Scandinavia, while running consistently through such sources there is the recurring element of music and poetry:

> John Morrison was the author of 'Dain Spioradail', 1828 and Iain Morrison, the poetic blacksmith of Rodel, died in 1852.

No matter how one views the veracity of family trees, the unmistakable Irish and Scottish cultural and social meshing of his own surname provides a myth of origin, which Van Morrison would explore in his music. Precious wonder too that his famous 1973-74 band and production company, Caledonia, should take its meaning from the Latin for northern Britain while Caledonian refers to a native of ancient Scotland. The cultural voyage, which Morrison undertook in the early 1970s, was in effect a journey back in time to such mythical beginnings.

At the age of five Van Morrison went to Elm Grove Primary School, a stone's throw away from his home at 125 Hyndford Street, just off the Beersbridge Road. The school banked on to Lady Dixon's playing fields; across the road, a clutch of streets with such pastoral names as Avoneil and Flora, and the historically laden Mayflower, while the Conn's Water ran through the district as a reminder of an earlier time when it gave its name to a small coastal port of some importance in the late sixteenth and seventeenth centuries.

Ballymacarrett, the townland, takes its name from the Gaelic, and means Town of Mac Art. It is a staunchly Protestant and loyalist area. Orange halls, band halls, working-men's clubs and bars and more recently, leisure and day centres, nursery schools and shopping malls front the redeveloped housing estates which settle alongside the numerous places of worship: Church of Ireland, Presbyterian, Methodist, Baptist, Non-Conformist and several evangelical sects, such as Jehovah Witnesses and Elim Pentecostal.

Morrison, like most of his contemporaries went to Sunday school and church. In the grand St. Donard's Church of Ireland at the Bloomfield intersection, barely ten minutes' walk from the leafy Cyprus Avenue and suburban North road, the setting for some of his great early lyrics, Morrison would have heard an austere lesson in Christian faith, duty and reserve. Whereas in the evangelical meetings, an energetic and Americanised version of the gospel would speak of a spirited mission of redemption, the Blood of the Lamb and joy in Christ.

Protestantism was everywhere. From the Union Jack flying above the Orange halls, to billboards proclaiming Proverbial wisdom from the Bible, to assemblies and religious instruction at school, it was impossible not to absorb the teaching and cultural values of the Protestant church. In working-class east Belfast, as in other working-class areas throughout the city, Protestantism was a very wide church indeed, embracing mainstream traditions such as Anglicanism, Presbyterianism and Methodism towards the distinctively evangelical.

Protestants often took an *à la carte* attitude to their worship. While membership of a particular church passed down through families, generation by generation, it was not uncommon for mothers, in particular, to shop around and send their children to different churches under the broad umbrella of Protestantism.

There was the 'respectable' Church of Ireland, a hint always of the upwardly mobile seeking a place alongside the satisfied burghers of the district; the down-to-earth Presbyterians who tended also towards the political; the somewhat introverted Methodists and a panoply of different sects and breakaway groups who asked for much more personal commitment from their flock. 'There is in Ulster', remarks Steve Bruce, 'a pietistic evangelical tradition which sees religion as an alternative to the ways of the world and which stresses the importance of avoiding worldly contamination. Especially strong in working-class areas, a gospel hall and Pentecostal tradition serves as a way out of the everyday world'.

The atmosphere of such gospel halls and evangelical meeting houses could not be more different from either the highbred Church of Ireland or the Presbyterian Scottish Gothic. Built on wastelands, in derelict sites of one kind or another, at corners and out-of-the-way places, the huts of the evangelical revivalist preachers attracted a small but steady flow of the curious and disenchanted. Over the years, such sects developed and grew and, with them, the faithful paid for and built tabernacles in which fully-flown Crusades took place along with open-air rallies.

It is interesting to note that the best-known evangelical preacher to come out of Northern Ireland, Ian Paisley, preached an invitation sermon on Christmas Sunday 1945 at the Ravenhill Evangelical Mission Church in working-class east Belfast before becoming pastor to that Church. Within his lifetime he was to create a new church, the Free Presbyterian Church, one of whose buildings straddles the Ravenhill Road and receives busloads of worshippers every week.

That said, the sects are, and always have been, a minority in Belfast. Among the working class, such sects are often seen as obsessive, dour and self-righteous. Their influence fades into the wider Calvinist atmosphere, which pervaded the city throughout the post-war period and well into the 60s. There was a governing ethos of Sabbatarian rule, when all forms of entertainment were frowned upon on a Sunday—public bars, clubs, parks, cinemas and (most) dancehalls were closed; television was not allowed; blinds were often pulled or curtains closed and it was considered improper to play on the streets. The lasting negative effects of such a puritanical society upon those who grew up in it are obviously profound and mark to the very core the individual sensibility. There is, however, another side to this story. For the dominant religious force of Protestantism also carried, in different forms again, a contradictory sense of poetic language and choral and lyrical music.

While the routines of an evangelical meeting might appear to be soulless in comparison with, say, the ceremony of Catholic Mass or the pomp of High Church, the language of 'being healed' and 'saved', the plain witness of one man's voice bearing testimony to finding the Lord, has a poignancy and theatricality all its own. Textually based upon the Old Testament, adamant in its fundamentalist convictions of right and wrong, sin and forgiveness, speaking out against self-deception, and seeking the Lord through being Born Again, the language and performance of such preachers provided as much entertainment as it did spiritual guidance. The Minister, or pastor, or preacher, brings his religion to the audience so that they might see the light as well as the error of their ways, and gain thereby a new security of whom and what they are, having found themselves through salvation.

The evangelical power of conversion and redemption is drenched in the imagery of a simpler life, spurning illusions and the allure of false gods. It is a forceful, dogmatic and profoundly individualistic faith, which earnestly wrestles with issues of 'Truth' and the pursuit of the transcendental as both are embodied in the everyday, working life.

Hardly surprising then that the district in which Morrison grew up should include a Calvin Street. Protestantism was after all not solely 'a religion' but the way of life. As Morrison's ironic understatement has it: 'We didn't go to church all the time, but it was a very churchy atmosphere in the sense that that's the way it is in Northern Ireland.'

If Protestantism was like the air one breathed, the ground one walked on was assumed to be British. Post-war Belfast was an emphatically British city. Belfast had a recent history in common with other British cities—from the war effort to the Blitz and the thousands of American GIs, to the Victory Parades and ration-books, while the city itself was marked with bomb sites and pre-fabricated houses.

There were the local connections with Scotland— geographical as much as industrial, personal and cultural— and the politico-economic associations and social identification between a majority of the Protestant community and the mainland, and a not insubstantial proportion of the Catholic community as well.

Leaving for work in Scotland and England (but less so in

Wales) was part of the Belfast way of life. There was the historical exchange within the British Isles as job opportunities fell inside the Ulster province and rose elsewhere. Men would travel and settle, sometimes taking their families with them; sometimes not. This 'internal' emigration with family members eventually establishing homes away from Belfast—in Glasgow, London, Leeds, Birmingham, Newcastle, Liverpool—was a fairly common practice since quite early on in the century. In my own family, for instance, my maternal grandfather moved to Canada and worked for many years there before moving to Nottingham; his wife's sister left Belfast in the 1920s and settled in London, to return only once every ten years, and her daughter left London in the 1960s, lived and worked in Belfast for some time before returning to London. Such journeying back and forth has followed personal needs and at the same time reflected upon wider economic and cultural pressures over the past century. This 'emigration' accelerated at various critical moments such as the Depression of the late 1920s and mid to late 30s with emigration further afield to Canada, America and Australia. More recently, from the early 1970s to the present, the twenty-five years of the Troubles, has seen an exodus, particularly among the young, a pattern which continues to this day, most noticeably among the Protestant middle-class.

It was not always thus, however. Workers could also travel *into* Northern Ireland, although it was a protected labour market, given the scandalously high unemployment figures of the province. Permits were required for anyone born outside to work inside. Be that as it may, there was a constant flow of workers back and forth across the Irish Sea. I recall meeting in 1986, at a Christmas party in suburban north London, the Scottish father of a very English hostess. He was in his eighties and had worked, he told me with ironic pride, on the building of Stormont, the Northern Ireland parliament buildings which were opened in 1932 by the then Prince of Wales (later Edward VIII).

The imposing neo-classical house of colonial parliament, visible from all over Belfast, dominates an impressively landscaped site on the Upper Newtownards Road in the east of the city. The old worker told me that there were many Scottish craftsmen who worked on the building, having been brought in especially from Glasgow, including gold leaf specialists whose artwork, originally used for the grand interiors of liners, can still be seen on the ceilings and cornices of this once all-powerful seat of central power.

Stormont's extended heyday was between 1932 and 1972 when the British Prime Minister, Edward Heath, suspended the Stormont government as a result of the rapidly deteriorating security and political situation in Northern Ireland. The building came to symbolise the ignominious failure of the provincial parliament. Its fifty years of political life since the partition in 1922 of Ireland had not addressed the religious and cultural divisions that were so potently marked in the north. While the economic basis of the state was deeply indebted to British investment, the British government in Westminster equally underwrote its educational and social welfare system.

For barely twenty years or so, in the post-World War II, pre-Troubles period, (roughly between the late 1940s and late 1960s) the provincial government had within its grasp the opportunity to redress the sense of injustice and discrimination many Catholics experienced throughout Northern Ireland, and in no place more keenly than Belfast.

That failure of political will was undeniably the key historical turning point. It acted like a catalyst to the sectarian warfare, political jingoism and paramilitary power struggles which would eventually claim the lives of over three thousand people and maim, physically and emotionally, hundreds of thousands of people in the north, the Republic, in Britain and elsewhere.

Yet most historians agree that the slow signs of prosperity which started to show in the local post-war Northern economy, with the shipyard employing 20,000 workers in 1959, and the steps being taken to better the living standards of ordinary people, were all linked in the public mind at least with the continued union of Northern Ireland as part of Britain. Schoolbooks, radio programmes, regional television when it eventually came (May 1955) accepted and underscored the status quo. There was an unquestionable belief that Belfast had weathered the storm and that it could look forward, in some manner of means, to an improved future, certainly if measured by pre-war standards.

A new Health system was inaugurated and in 1947 the Education Act established, amongst other items, free public secondary intermediate education. This would take all children from 5 to 15 years of age. The grammar school sector expanded somewhat to cope with the rising lower middle-class aspirations and further education centres opened. To a young boy, moving between home, school and just knocking around, such concerns were irrelevant. It seems clear that to Van Morrison the main preoccupation of his childhood years was music. This would not have been uncommon either.

Throughout working-class Belfast different forms of music proliferate, particularly *playing* music. Often associated with ceremonial occasions, a tradition exists of flute bands, silver bands and military bands which filled the air not only during the marching seasons of July through to August, but, throughout the year, band practice was an accepted and regular meeting place. This tradition is extensive and has been subject to very little research but much misunderstanding.

For the Orange party tunes—like the rebel songs of the Nationalist tradition—form only one part, and a greatly fluctuating part, in the tradition as a whole. The tunes of these different kinds of bands vary greatly from hymns to ballads to popular 'classics', (title-tracks from television programmes, for example) to marching tunes.

The principle of selection has generally been what is popular at any given time, along with the ceremonial music drawn from the British military tradition: from 'Rock of Ages' to 'Z Cars' to a Beatles number to 'The Dam Busters' to a sentimental Percy French melody for good measure.

As the Rev. Gary Hastings, an authority on northern musical traditions, explained to me, the great desire of late nineteenth and twentieth century northern Protestant marching music was for respectability; a demonstration of community discipline and self-regard modelled along military lines.

Having moved from the infantryman's fife-and-drum to the civilian flute, snare drum, Scottish pipes, accordion, (and very rarely, the powerful lambeg drum), the band music provided a cultural backdrop to life in Northern Ireland. Its message was double-edged: on the one hand, it was simply music to be played for its own sake and heartily enjoyed. On the other hand, it was 'Protestant' music insofar as it maintained, on particular public and state occasions, cultural distinctions between that community and their fellow Catholic northerners. It was a music played on the streets and in the parks; broadcast on the radio and featured in church. Indeed, as Gary Hastings pointed out, the role of the church in maintaining public interest in ceremonial music is central. For in one Protestant church, or church hall, after another, religion and entertainment met.

Furthermore, through the socialising role of its own organisations, such as the Boys' and Girls' Brigade, the Scouting Movement and so forth, the language, imagery and morality of Bible, Faith and Empire meshed into one common fabric. The church, in other words, was a social place and music played an absolutely crucial role in unifying the community.

Again there are differences within the broad Protestant faith. As the Rev. Hastings described it, the upbeat, clapping, and religious 'come-all-ye's' of the evangelical fundamentalist sects, which grew out of Ulster, contrast sharply with the Church of Ireland, and its organ-based, choral hymn-singing and remote and thoughtful rituals.

At a much more practical level, of course, with so many bandsmen and bandswomen in the community as a whole— for the Catholic community responded with its own orders, religious and cultural societies, and its own bands and days of celebration—the pool of musicians with basic playing skills and knowledge of music was quite extensive, given the actual population of Belfast and the province at large.

This dominant civic music, powerful and popular as it has been throughout the brief history of the Northern Ireland state, could not totally eclipse 'the tiny musical survivals' (the phrase is the Rev. Hastings') of an older tradition, a folk music. This technically astute and intensive music, played on the fiddle, flute, melodeon, uillean pipes, bodhran, was basically dancing music. When sung, it usually retold sad stories of love lost, emigration or praise for a beloved local place.

It is an exciting music, driven by powerful but simple repetitive rhymes. Unlike the, relatively speaking, mass involvement of marching bands, the individual fiddler, flute-player or piper addresses a closed audience of fellow-musicians, listeners or a set of dancers. Even the formal concert setting seems unnatural.

The roots of the music are rural and before the advent of radio or television traditional music was the form of musical entertainment. But with the explosion of musical options which came in the wake of World War II and the much wider availability of radio, cinema, and eventually television, the tradition went underground. Individual musicians scattered, often in search of work in the cities elsewhere in Ireland, Britain and North America. Like blues-guitarists and musicians, if they travelled away from home, they either fell silent or kept within their own ethnic communities. Audiences at home shrank as the new forms of orchestrated popular music took over in the late 1940s and 1950s.

Ciaran Mac Mathuna, a leading collector of Irish folk music, reminds us of the time when in Ireland, 'middle-class people laughed at this kind of [traditional] music, when it was considered just good enough for the countryside, and when city people and the middle class didn't like or didn't want to know about this music'. Back in the 1950s and 60s', Mac Mathuna recalls, 'on a long dance late in the night, [the band] might have thrown in an Irish dance for a bit of a laugh, but that was all'.

Belfast was different in that, during the early 60s, as the twenty-four year old Morrison described it in an interview published in *Rolling Stone* in July 1970, there was an important, if limited, crossover taking place in the city:

> Memphis Slim has been in Belfast; Jessie Fuller, Champion Jack Dupree, John Lee Hooker's been there. They've got folk clubs and rock clubs there, but it's got nothing to do with the English scene. In fact, I'd go so far as to say it doesn't have much to do with the Irish scene either, it's just Belfast. It's got its own identity, it's got its own people ... it's just a different race, a different breed of people. There's a lot of changes there, too. Like the McPeak[e]'s on one hand, and some others of us on the other hand, and they're open to all kinds of music, not just one thing. Maybe a third of the people that are into R&B would go to hear the McPeak[e]s.

Morrison has also referred in other interviews to his having started off 'in folk music' which can be taken as shorthand for the singer/musician as an individual who first learns and then puts his or her individual stamp on what has gone before. A further interesting note from the 1970 interview is Morrison seeing blues and traditional Irish music as essentially linked in the context of Belfast of the previous decade. The imaginative shift from Irish traditional music to blues and jazz that seemed quite natural in Morrison's recollection of the late 50s and early 1960s had begun to show political strains by the early 1970s. Travelling around the city and becoming increasingly more interested in traditional music, I became aware of the growing ghettoisation of the music, despite the best efforts of many of the musicians and a substantial part of the audience as well. Morrison's good fortune was to have encountered traditional Irish music without the politico-cultural freight it was expected to deal with during the next twenty years.

More importantly, though, there was the very early exposure to what Morrison has continuously acknowledged as the key influence of his early years in Belfast: his father. 'There was probably only 10 big collectors [of blues and jazz] in Belfast and [my father] was one of them.'

Alongside these recordings played to the young Morrison, he has spoken about his mother's singing—'I'll Take You Home Again, Kathleen', 'Sweet Sixteen' and 'Irene Goodnight'—as well as the popular ballads of the day. 'Whatever was on the radio.'

It was coincidental, of course, that during the 1950s Britain was experiencing a skiffle and trad jazz revival, inspired in part by the blues played by American blacks. Morrison has often cited his days playing 'in a skiffle group' and his having 'started off in folk music'. The historical picture has been drawn in detail by musicologists such as Charlie Gillet in *The Sound of the City*, Lawrence Cohn in *Nothing But the Blues* and by participants like George Melly in *Revolt into Style*.

Belfast was no exception, and many of the leading lights of the trad jazz revival played concerts in Belfast during the mid to late 1950s. Witness, for example, the English poet, Philip Larkin, who lived and worked as a librarian at Queen's University, as he recalls in the introduction to his record diary *All What Jazz* (1968), the following scene in the Plaza ballroom, Chichester Street, Belfast. It is 1954:

> A thousand people squashed into the smallish Plaza dance hall and a thousand more milled outside, the more enterprising getting in through a small square window in the

men's lavatory ... Lonnie Donegan would come forward with his impersonation of Leadbelly.

Nine-year-old Morrison was back home in Hyndford Street listening to the original records of Leadbelly, an artist whom Morrison much later was to identify as one of the strongest earliest influences upon him, along with other great blues artists such as Muddy Waters, Sonny Terry and Brownie McGhee. George Melly's point in *Revolt into Style* is well worth bearing in mind too, when he writes about the violent world of which Leadbelly sang. 'Leadbelly was in prison twice on murder charges and had a near psychopathic personality. Donegan's version was safely distanced from that world. Its violence and harshness was make-believe and in retrospect he sounds more like George Formby than Huddie Ledbetter.'

The connection made at such an early age might also account for the emphasis, which Morrison had alluded to in interviews, with the emotional bonds and cultural aspirations many Belfast people shared with North America as much as with Britain.

In the early 1950s, Morrison's father visited America, worked there for a time and considered moving his wife and son there. It was also during this period that Morrison has said he became hooked on the radio, listening to Voice of America and clearly the young Morrison's exposure at such an early age to real blues could only have a profound and lasting effect.

It is well worth noting the afterglow in Belfast of the 1950s left by the many American troops, including black GIs, who had been stationed throughout the north. Having brought with them not only bubblegum and cigarettes but their own styles of music and dance, they took over the floor of ballrooms such as the Plaza (built in 1942) with, for Belfast, an uncharacteristic flamboyance and glamour.

Undoubtedly the Belfast that Morrison knew growing up was split-levelled. There was the orthodox, self-satisfied official exterior, as formidable as the City Hall itself, expecting its citizens to believe that all was well and that things could only get better, particularly for the city's loyal sons and daughters.

On the other hand, there were also throughout the city men and women such as George and Violet Morrison, and their son, Ivan, whose primary interest was simply in music. It was an alternative world, which ultimately permeated the pieties and structure of the known and accepted society experiencing, as it then was in the mid-1950s, something of an upswing and expansion, including the widening provision of educational opportunities.

One of the new schools established around this time, in 1957, and officially opened the following year (May 3rd, 1958) was Orangefield Boys' School. It was subsequently joined by a Girls' School and on the same site, by Grosvenor Grammar school, originally located on Grosvenor Road since 1945.

Orangefield's headmaster was a dynamic yet cool-tempered scholar called John Malone. He was a liberal who had fought against the staid and complacent educational authorities in Belfast. He sought to build in Orangefield a genuinely comprehensive education for working-class children of east Belfast. The school curriculum, however, was to include not only the standard grounding in applied trades and clerkly professions that most, if not all, of its students would eventually join. It also set out to encourage a wider—some would say, experimental—learning in music, theatre, politics, and, of course, sport. The school would also provide a social focus.

The school's young and more experienced teachers alike supported Malone's vision. His beliefs were, however, to be severely tested given the deep-seated cultural prejudices of the 1950s and early 1960s. Work was considered to be the logical and only reason for educating ordinary working-class boys and girls. This was in keeping with the dominant religious and political ethos of Protestant unionism of the time as well. Orangefield conceded, indeed actively endorsed, these principles in naming the four school 'houses'—or fraternities—after local engineering works such as Sirocco and Bryson.

However, as the school soon established itself by the mid-1960s, it had achieved an academic recognition beyond the original remit and throughout the 60s was identified as Belfast's leading progressive 'comprehensive' school, with pupils of quite diverse backgrounds attending from all over the city, alongside those drawn from the immediate catchment area of east Belfast. We catch a glimpse of this fission when Morrison describes his years at Orangefield (1956-1960):

> There was no school for people like me. I mean, we were freaks in the full sense of the word because either we didn't have the bread to go to the sort of school where we could sit down and do our thing, or that type of school didn't exist. Most of what was fed me really didn't help me that much later.

While things were to change at that very school in a matter of a few years, Morrison had moved on by then.

Given, however, the conservatism, snobbery and civic priorities of Belfast in the mid to late 1950s it is hardly surprising that Morrison, along with others of his own age, should look for something else. Blues music became that voice of dissent but it was fundamentally an emotional reaction, not a political act. Black musicians like Leadbelly, Jelly Roll Morton, and jazz figures like Charlie Parker embodied a way of life and represented a kind of lifestyle with which the young Morrison could identify.

From early on, he had picked up a guitar bought for him by his father. Armed with his guitar, Morrison obviously found himself, as did so many others of that time and since, with his fate literally in his hands. Within no time, he was playing and imitating the records he had been listening to and looking for the chance to perform. The crucial difference with Morrison, as the years between the late 1950s and 1967, when he left Belfast, clearly show, is that he was not only discovering a powerfully-focused talent; he was also encountering the world through his music and the subculture of which it was to be the all-embracing focus. If playing music was just a job, as he had repeatedly said, it was some job.

> The original idea in the British Isles was just to get out of your working-class environment and make a living out of playing music. It's that simple. I just wanted to be a musician, full-time. That was the ultimate goal (*Q.* 1993).

Precious wonder that in his later work, of the 1980s and 90s, Morrison would seek to imaginatively rediscover through his music again that early home from whence it had all started. The mature Morrison's realisation is chastened, however, by the fact that it was his very talent which had cast him out in the first place. Morrison's lyrics are driven by that sense of contradiction: the intimacy and quietude of home is shaken by doubt and uncertainty about its ability to sustain the demands of the artistic and professional world beyond. Morrison's work as musician and singer-songwriter negotiates this tension, whether that is in the intensely lyrical passages of *Astral Weeks* (1968), the rage of 'Listen to the Lion' (1974) or in his most recent work of the 1990s from *Hymns to the Silence* (1991) to the present.

There was the traditional east Belfast route, apprenticed to one of the local engineering works such as Musgrave & Co. When this proved unsatisfactory, Morrison worked in a meat-cleaning factory, in a chemist's shop and went freelance, cleaning windows around the Orangefield area. Each job was secondary to the real business of playing with the ever-changing line-ups of local bands, from Deanie Sands and The Javelins, later The Thunderbolts, to their final formation in 1960 when they became The Monarchs. His professional career can be said to start from the early gigs with The Monarchs with whom he played saxophone.

The popular musical background throughout Ireland at this time in the early 60s, north and south, was the dominance of dancehall showbands, antiseptic ceildhe music and pub-based folk, modelled on and derived from groups like the Clancy Brothers. The showband scene was an ersatz mixture of cover versions of 'pop' hits from America and England. Whatever about his private education in blues and jazz, Morrison had to work his way through the current reality of audience expectations at the time. The fall-out of the trad-jazz revival in the 1950s, more or less petered out, had returned to minority status, along with Irish traditional music and folk singing.

There was, however, an additional influence at play in that Morrison was starting to make connections through his reading with the work of the Beat generation, in particular the iconic autobiographical novel, *On the Road* (1958) written by Jack Kerouac.

Kerouac's fiction such as *On the Road* and *Dharma Bums* (1959) are roads to freedom as the group of fugitives spurn the white, puritanical, work-obsessed post-war America of their own time for a life of self-obsessed experimentation and indeterminate future on the west coast.

Kerouac also wrote aggressively in his own voice, a style of conversational address, buoyed up with jazz-talk and immediate access to poetic vision:

> It was a wonderful night. Central City is two miles high; at first you get drunk on the altitude, then you get tired, and there's a fever in your soul. We approached the lights around the opera house down the narrow dark street; then we took a sharp right and hit some old saloons with swinging doors. Most of the tourists were in the opera. We started off with a few extra-size beers. There was a player piano. Beyond the back door was a view of mountainsides in the moonlight. I let out a yahoo. The night was on.

For the intense teenager, hanging out in Belfast, these words must have sounded like a new gospel. As George Jones remarked: 'He wrote poetry. It was deep ... most of us didn't know what he was talking about.' Kerouac's reverence for jazz, too, would not have gone amiss, as black blues artists and the mention of poet figures such as Rimbaud could only inspire Morrison in undoubtedly the same way as it had earlier influenced Bob Dylan and The Doors singer, Jim Morrison, among a generation who were discovering Kerouac for the first time.

It is of course all too easy with hindsight to see, in those first few years of the 1960s, Morrison gathering into himself the professional experience needed to maintain a 'career' as a musician. Much more importantly, he was forming the attitudes and belief in himself that such a life was actually possible. There can be no inevitability about such desires, as if Morrison planned his career step by step. Far from it. He moved where and when he could and took what chances came his way, something he has been quite clear about himself:

> Picture the situation. Put yourself working in showbands, touring in buses with seven or eight people, sleeping in parks, having no money. Put yourself through working the clubs in Germany, on up to when the R&B movement thing was happening in the 60s; put yourself through being in a situation where you're supposed to be a somebody. The thing that has carried me through this is the time I put in when I was nobody. When I was with Them, it was anti-climactic. All right so I'm a star but I don't want it. I just do my music.

In an effort to secure more gigs the five-man Monarchs added four musicians to their original line-up and became a showband. This meant that while they were no longer 'a group' they could now play in the bigger Belfast ballrooms. The four-piece band (drums, bass, lead guitar and singer) was supplemented with keyboards and brass instruments.

One of the new additions, Ronnie Osborne, had joined from a brass band. The Monarchs were in effect caught between two worlds and the next year and more tells a fascinating story of musical aspirations confronting show-business reality. The ballroom requirements were simple: play the music that the audience was hearing on the radio and buying records of in the shops. They were there to dance; the band was there to entertain. After all, dancing was a night out. The ballrooms themselves were imitation palaces; the showbands were dressed up in distinctive monogrammed liveries (a crown for The Monarchs) that fell somewhere between quasi-military uniforms (underlined by the somewhat mechanical dance-steps on stage) and formal wedding attire. The showbands also provided flashes of showmanship within an ongoing, self-contained and predictable musical set. The music was all about polish and the majority of the musicians were highly skilled in imitating all sorts of music. Their inner musical inclinations were quite firmly subservient to the wishes of the audience, ballroom owner and promoter. While some 'hotter' numbers could be smuggled in to become breathing spaces between dances, or to show off one of the band's players, in the main they replicated 'hits', irrespective of whether they were pop, country & western or 'jokey' ballads:

> May the bird of paradise fly up your nose;
> May an elephant caress you with its toes.

As George Jones told journalist Vincent Power, 'There was no other outlet'. Morrison's own comments underscore the commercial realities of the time: 'You couldn't work properly if you didn't have [a horn section]. All the showbands had horn sections and a lot of them were really good, like the Royal Showband, the Dixielanders, the Swingtime Aces, Clipper Carlton.'

So what The Monarchs were doing in 1960, ahead of time, was including in their repertoire, alongside the pop material, some material from the R&B American style of Ray Charles and Muddy Waters. Given the times that were in it, such innovation was a risky business but frustrating nonetheless for Morrison who obviously wanted to push further into that terrain.

After a spell away from The Monarchs, Morrison and the by-now seven-piece band decided to have a go and travelled to Scotland in 1962. Behind them there were five years or so of playing the dance halls and ballrooms of their own locality—Belfast and the surrounding counties. Now they had left this behind them, albeit only in Scotland, the harsher realities of being away from home, on the road and looking for work must have pressed in upon the unlikely group of lads. It is a story told many times since of prospecting, buoyed up with the two Glaswegians whom they had met in Belfast, the Belfast group travelled around Scotland expecting more work than they could actually find, and so they decided to travel south to London.

This is the stuff of myth making, of course: the provincial encounters with the cosmopolitan culture that was such a defining feature of the 'Swinging Sixties': pop culture, literature, film and theatre. As George Jones recounts, they drove directly to London from Aberdeen: 'We were really tired. We just kept driving to try and find a place to bunk down. We felt dejected. We were ready to go home, but didn't want to give in to our parents.' All teenagers, The Monarchs were in London in 1962 in a van. What they had going for them was their own selves and the knowledge and feeling for a different kind of music. It was to sustain the group for a year or so, including a tour of Britain and

Germany, before their return to Belfast in 1963. This was an absolutely crucial time for Morrison's development because between these years (1962-67) he would be confronted by both the commercial exigencies of the music business but also begin the real struggle for his own artistic independence, an abiding theme of his work ever since.

Morrison records at the very heart of his work a series of dilemmas. He has spoken of these in the interviews he has given throughout a career which now spans forty and more years, interviews which reveal Morrison as a vastly experienced and uncompromising critic of the contemporary world and the fate within it of genuine artistic endeavour.

As a musician, all Morrison need do is entertain (what he calls 'earning my living') but there is also a profound desire to communicate more than that; as a performer, there is the conflict between protecting the individual private self while dealing with, and in, a mass market music business which thrives on, and exploits, disclosure. There is, too, the never-ending struggle for balance as Morrison's music aspires to some form of genuine spiritual experience while simultaneously contending with the rigours, routines and business of touring with a band. Running through these emotionally charged and intently artistic issues, Morrison's writing lights upon the imagery of Protestant mysticism while the songs, reaching for rapture, recollect human limitation and loss against which his voice and lyrics protest.

Morrison's time with Them was the brief use of direct musical force. The band, formed in Belfast late in 1963, captured the mood of the city. Indeed from this period in the early 1960s, Belfast was to produce a number of bands who

Van Morrison's Them *captured the mood of 60s Belfast.*

played a mix of R&B and blues. They lived on stage performances, as Morrison has made clear many times, at such venues as Belfast's Maritime Hotel. As a live band, the energy of their performances was not captured in the singles, such as 'Don't Start Crying Now', 'Baby Please Don't Go', 'Gloria' (1964), 'Here Comes the Night' (1965) or the albums they released, *Them* (1965) and *Them Again* (1966).

The raw, almost belligerent energy of Morrison's voice spoke directly of and to a generation coming into its own during the early 1960s. But there was much more involved than brash display. In 'The Story of Them', written by Morrison, the narrative recounts a Belfast literally opening out, as 'Blues come rolling down Royal Avenue/Won't stop by the City Hall/Just a few steps away/You can look up at The Maritime Hotel'.

Morrison's searching elaboration of the syllables of his tale is mocked by the quizzing lead guitar as the emerging generation in the actual story stares back at the world with bristling self-preoccupation. 'The Story of Them' is a mini-epic sung to the laid-back rhythms of talking blues:

> When friends were friends and company was right
> We'd drink and talk and sing all through the night
> And morning came leisurely and bright.
> Down town we'd walk and passers-by
> Would shudder with delight. Hmnn—Good times.

The languor of Morrison's voice is underscored by the band's consistently fugitive and disconsolate backing. The characteristic note is of a past that has slipped away: 'It was a gas'. The instant retake on the band's life on the stage of the Maritime tells a rhetorical story about defiance and disdain ('We don't care') which is dramatised through the inflections of Morrison's Belfast accent. As he plays with individual words like 'Look' and toys with occasional harmonica rushes, Morrison's voice evokes an imaginative terrain that is in the mind's eye, summoned by the names and sounds of places and things:

> Barred from pubs, clubs and dancing halls
> Made the scene at the Spanish Rooms on the Falls
> And then four pints of that scrumpy was enough to have you
> out of your mind, climbing up the walls, out of your mind.

Acknowledging the help of 'The Three Jays'—Jerry McKenna, Jerry McKervey and Jimmy Conlon, young promoters on the music scene in the early 1960s—Morrison laments, 'It was something else then'. With a surprising lack of sentimentality or nostalgia, questions are asked and answered in an impersonation of the audience's view of what they, the audience, are looking at on stage. 'The Story of Them' is Morrison in dramatic monologue:

> People say, 'Who are Them?' Or 'What are Them?'

> That little one sings and that big one plays the guitar
> With a thimble on his finger, runs it up and down the strings;
> Bass player don't say much:
> I think they are all a little bit touched.

The colloquial idiom of 'a little bit touched' runs alongside the self-consciousness of the whole number and the ambiguous, contradictory relationship between band and audience, time and place is summed up in the simple declaration:

> Wild, sweaty, crude, ugly and mad,
> Sometimes just a little bit sad.
> Yeah, they sneered and all,
> but up there we were just having a ball.
> We are Them, take it or leave it.
> Do you know they took it,
> and they kept coming.

Morrison departs the songs, 'just a little bit sad/gonna walk for a while/wish it well'. A gesture which features in so many of his lyrics as the insider leaves with the knowledge that to return is ever afterwards always going to be qualified by the fact of leaving.

What is clear from the recordings of Morrison with Them is the self-belief and confidence in what they are doing on stage. As he says in 'The Story of Them', 'The people kept coming'. In the Maritime, and the other small clubs around Belfast, an audience was building up for the peculiar mix of blues, R&B and a folk-jazz reminiscent of Dylan. This growing audience, mainly young, working class and lower-middle class, had previously been invisible. They were children of the Welfare state and the first generation to really benefit from the steady if slow upswing in economic fortunes during the late 1950s and the early 1960s. According to David Harkness, 'Material conditions improved for many in both communities in these years, and many began to move into new housing areas where religions intermingled and good neighbours were found amongst traditional foes'. Notwithstanding what Harkness also refers to as the 'ingrained unemployment problem', which afflicted the northern economy, the mid-1960s reflected, at least on the surface, an image of the provincial capital as vibrant and in touch with what was going on in the world.

Variously billed as Belfast's Jazz Club and Rhythm & Blues Club, the Maritime Hotel in College Square North was a Merchant Seaman's Hostel built (on the site of a former Royal Irish Constabulary station) in 1945 by the British Sailors Society.

Situated with its back ironically shunning two of the city's most famous educational institutes, the Royal Belfast Academical Institution ('Inst') and the College of Technology, and equidistant between the city centre and the bottom of the Falls Road, the Club in 1964 was the focus for Queen's University students and the outward-going and confident working class young.

In this most work-orientated of cities, where status and prestige were intrinsically linked to one's 'steady' job and prospects (or lack of both), the students had an identity of their own. In meeting up with those working-class kids in their late teens or early twenties, a brief crossover took place that was to last during the midyears of the 1960s. In passing, it's true to say that as things were to develop, with the eruption of the Troubles in the late 60s and early 70s, the

Maritime, alongside other 'clubs' such as Sammy Houston's in Great Victoria Street, provided a chance for kids of every religion and none to get together. Such thoughts would have been far from the minds of those at the time, however; all that mattered was the music.

For many working-class kids, seeing students look like 'beatniks' would have had a greater effect on them than wondering about which church they went to. The experience must have been something of a liberation from the conventions of previous generations when 'going out' meant dressing 'proper'. For the general rule had been that once the dungarees, factory overalls or shop clothes were taken off, it was time to 'dress up'.

The men, older brothers and uncles, next-door neighbours, with their hair quiffed and immaculately cut; aftershaved; a thin bar of white handkerchief in the breast-pocket of the Burton's Italian suit, the required showing of cuff with the monogrammed links and gleaming Chelsea boots; their girls in dresses and imitation furs or 'swag coats' always carrying in their handbags the silver dagger-like back-combing comb to ensure the look. Men would also always carry a comb in their breast or back pocket. A Friday or Saturday night was the chance to be part of a picture-show in which everyone who ventured out had style and became an actor. Belfast's city centre, with the light spilling out from the plate-glass shopfront windows and the perpetual flow of buses, was actually like a stage set for drama. And drama there was. Lovers met 'down town', had drinks, and went to the pictures or to a classy ballroom.

There could be bloody and at time vicious fist-fights, and worse, for the macho, vain or vanquished in this most intensely proud and symbolic display of male proprieties. Women would sometimes imitate.

There could be operatic rows between dates in shop doorways or at street corners and on buses. Indeed, to circumnavigate Belfast's city centre on a weekend was often an experience in itself. For it was to watch (but not too intently for fear of ending up involved!) the clash between the theatrical and the everyday. Working life confronted itself with time off and was exposed in turn to the dream world of entertainment, leisure and possibility. A world, it was commonly believed, which 'the students' perpetually inhabited.

With their 'long' hair, wearing whatever came their way from duffle coats to old school blazers, flared pants, old ex-army leather jackets, polo necks, jeans, suede shoes and Norfolk coats, the students defied (if only for a few years) the working ethos of the city. They were an unknown quantity and, in a sense, Queen's students of the time lived in a quarantined world. They had a fool's pardon when they ventured through the city centre and would have been treated with short shrift during the mid-1960s had they made their presence felt at the ballrooms and larger dancehalls whose audiences were, to a man and woman, working hard for the rest of the week. This was also true of some of the city bars.

It's hardly surprising, therefore, that the students would find their own venues such as the Maritime. From being a venue for variety-type concerts as well as trad jazz, the Maritime became synonymous with R&B, the music which symbolised a breaking away from, and loosening of, custom. On the ground floor a café faced up to a flight of stairs, and along the narrow institutional-like painted passageway, there was a small dancehall. It had a small stage and bands would often walk through the audience to reach it, or, having finished their set, simply jump down from the stage and mill about with the audience. They played short sets of half an hour to forty minutes, local band following local band, or sometimes a visiting band. Belfast was very much part of the British circuit and most of the well-known and not so well known bands of the time played the city.

The Maritime had, however, enough of its own bands to turn over two or three each night. They looked like their audiences and did whatever they fancied on stage; smoking and drinking. The Maritime was breaking down the expected notion of musical entertainment as something that is 'provided by' an ensemble of musicians into something created between themselves and the audience.

No showband uniforms here or spangling glacial mirrors. The formal paired dancing of the ballrooms, even the riskier jive, gave way, and at other similar clubs, to solo expression, body to body, which had a sexual frankness well beyond the sophisticated flirting and masquerade of showband music. No wonder I can recall the excitement of a friend's older sister telling us about this 'brilliant' dance club and then demurring in front of her mother about whether or not it would be a fit place for boys 'our age'. So that by the time we had moved into the Maritime, just after Them had broken up, and it had become Club Rado, the name of the Maritime was synonymous with excitement and risk and a sense of being part of a generation.

It was in actual fact an extraordinarily confined space with people crammed everywhere. Bands such as Sam Mahood & The Just Five religiously maintained the R&B

Them, 'Ready, Steady, Go', 1964.
Van Morrison, Pat McAuley, Alan Henderson, Billy Harrison,
John McAuley.

ethos, while the slightly more college-based blues of The Few was clearly indebted to John Mayall, a regular visitor to the city with his Bluesbreakers, and the fervent Soul of The Interns. Later on Rory Gallagher and Taste played regularly at the Club.

Added to this 'tradition' of a few years' standing, imported bands were eager to play at the Maritime but their showmanship often superseded musical skills. Arthur Brown's Experience, who arrived on stage with a headpiece on fire to sing 'Fire', comes to mind.

In April 1964, when Morrison and Them first played the Maritime, the atmosphere would have been significantly different because the band and audience were part of something that was new. The exhilaration of the music that Them played was substantially a part of rejecting the established 'pop' music of the time, particularly in Ireland.

Sam Mahood, the irrepressible soul man.

Dublin had 'pop' and 'soul' bands as indeed had Belfast. But Morrison's voice, Them's music, dress and mannerisms were guaranteed to satisfy a feeling for rebellious self-assertion: what *against* was left to one side. The aggression is caught in the sound of the music; even when the song is of love lost, the regret is tinged with anger. Them played a style of R&B that was not only good to dance to but was also conscious of itself. Being a fan of Them, as listening to R&B for a generation, was subtly identifying oneself: in Belfast of that time, it carried the aura of being anti-establishment, with the Maritime as the cavernous symbol.

The anthem of that identification was 'Gloria', the flipside of 'Baby Please Don't Go', Them's second single, released in England in November 1964. The band had been playing for barely eight months but had now a record in the British charts, and an appearance on the prestigious Independent Television's 'Ready Steady Go' programme. Confirmation of their status came with the decision to use 'Baby Please Don't Go' as the programme's title music. Albeit with critical hindsight, it is true to say that Morrison's writing for 'Gloria' had found a perfect pitch: an aggressive and physical lyric which moves, literally step-by-step, towards sexual encounter. The almost martial drumming which Morrison breaks into with his story, 'Like to tell you 'bout my baby', is urgent in its portrait of a midnight world:

> She comes walking down my street,
> Won't you come to my house
> She knocks upon my door
> And then she comes to my room
> Then she makes me feel alright.

The subjective territory of the song is stressed very much in the possessive—'my' street, 'my' house, 'my' door and 'my' room. The link between street life and inner sanctum is hypnotically cast as the girl's name is spelt out: G.L.O.R.I.A. Whatever about the speculations as to who 'Gloria' actually was (a fate which pursues many of Morrison's lyrics, most famously 'Madame George') the focus is on the man and not the woman. That is what the shouting is all about. It were as if the singer was actually on the street, calling; not uncommon in Belfast.

The echoey, sparse sound of 'Gloria' may well be the first 'punk' record, as some maintain. For Morrison is, after all, writing out of a vibrant local idiom, which prizes brash, almost interrogative, frankness. This did indeed involve calling out names and provocatively drawling vowels, as much as a summons as a celebration. In the back of the song, too, the skipping tunes accompanying street games is not too far away from the emphatic rhythms, but transformed by the band from kids' stuff into passion. All the more important, therefore, to recall, by way of contrast, the tone of suburban ennui and middle-class complacency which sickens the young Gavin Burke in Brian Moore's highly regarded Belfast-based novel, *The Emperor of Ice Cream* (1965).

Set in Belfast of the 1940s, Moore's portrait of the city as 'this dull, dead town' remained a dominant cultural stereotype. Thwarted in love, disillusioned by narrow politics, put off by the self-consciously 'arty' set of his hometown, Gavin only finds redemption in the apocalyptic blitz in which he (heroically) finds himself at last. In contrast, Sam Hanna Bell's *The Hollow Ball* (1961) tells a somewhat different kind of love story:

> They decided on a walk in the Botanic Gardens before going downtown. The sun dropping behind the Castlereagh Hills glittered on the pastel coats of the women, the starched collars of the respectable young men, the diamanté ornament in Maureen's fur collar. There was a tingle in the air that pierced their hands and turned their laughter to smoke. At the entrance to the new rose garden he caught her hand and they fled under the rustic arches, past the children and the dogs, past the gaping park attendant fumbling in his memory for a by-law that restrained young men and pretty girls from running in the winter sunlight, past the rude young men hooting at them from the shelter by the bandstand.

What Bell is hinting at here, and what his novel overall dramatises, is the up and down sides of life in Belfast. The important thing is that, according to Bell, there was an upside, in the first place! The parks, the evening sunlight, the sexual joy and innocence, the music and, even while shadowed by that authority figure of the 'park attendant', there is that pronounced lyrical feeling of possibility. This is where Morrison comes in, with a vision all of his own conveyed through the exuberance of his voice.

With the demise of Them, after a time touring in England and in the States, Morrison's lyrics become preoccupied with what looks like a contradiction. For as Morrison discovers a rich thematic seam in writing about the Belfast he had grown up in, at the very same time, living in Belfast was frustrating him. 'As far as ideas and stuff were concerned', he told Richie York, 'America was the place for me. That's the way it worked out ... For Belfast, my ideas were too far out.'

Leaving Belfast in 1967 for New York, the twenty-one

year old Morrison displayed not only tremendous courage but a forthright belief in his own artistic vision. As he remarked in an interview in 1987: 'All I did from the time I was eighteen to twenty-seven was work. I worked my way from Belfast to New York and didn't even know I was there because it was work.'

Like Bob Dylan leaving Hibbing, Minnesota, at the turn of the decade, Morrison was willing to use whatever he wanted to make up his own tradition out of diverse musical influences and literally forge a different kind of music. An iconoclastic individualism which, even to this day, has caused problems because it has to be sustained in the teeth of one of, if not *the*, most heartless of industries, the music industry. That confrontation is a key to understanding Morrison's lyrics—the battle for survival, aligned with his temperamental and critical reading of the media and pop culture, from MTV, 'the fame game', to what he has called 'The Great Deception', which feeds off the music scene.

'It all comes down to survival,' Morrison is quoted as saying in an interview with *Rolling Stone* (1990), 'and you can't intellectualise survival, because either you survive or you don't. That's the way life goes, and I'm not going to intellectualise it, because that's only going to spoil it.'

In 1968, having behind him years of playing with several bands from the Javelins and Monarchs to Them, working in Ireland, Scotland and England, touring Germany and America, Morrison made in *Astral Weeks* an imaginative repossession of his own past and the language and landscapes associated with it.

Much has been made about this early album of Morrison's; justly so. It is important, however, to recall that like any performer, Morrison inhabits the stage as much as his work exists as recordings. The changing venues, musical contexts and audience expectations, place the live performance in the realm of theatre, with the band as cast. As Morrison said: 'An album is roughly forty minutes of music, that's all'. There is in Morrison's work the feeling that the lyric sound is more important than the written song. The voice dominates what is sung because language turns into music at certain points; the tongue, the throat, the making of sound is its own instrument. Morrison was later to imitate pipe music as a mantra; an incantation that plays with the adequacy of language to convey feeling.

In *Astral Weeks* there is a sense of what Sean O'Hagan accurately calls Morrison 'stretching the bounds of vocal expression to the limit'. This spontaneous yet experimental desire was very much part of the Beat Generation of the 50s and early 60s. As already mentioned, Morrison came in contact with Jack Kerouac and Allen Ginsberg through his reading. The influence of Kerouac, along with Ginsberg and Gary Synder, was, as the Beat Generation historian Anne Charters pointed out, central in linking poetry and jazz together in an attempted New Vision, tracking back to Blake and Walt Whitman and also into Rimbaud and D.H. Lawrence.

In Morrison's situation, however, the controlling principle of his music is underscored by an inherited suspicion of artistic looseness. Morrison's poetic free form has never been excess but access; a contest between passion and restraint. Unlike the Beat poets' critique of American consumer culture, there is not the faintest interest in identifying alternative political or social mores in Morrison's writing. His songs are about rapture, not radicalism.

The eight tracks of *Astral Weeks*, recorded in two days in New York and released in the US in November 1968, present a reverie: a consistent personal dramatisation of mood, landscape, romantic longing and nostalgia for a lost Eden. *Astral Weeks* explores this earlier age of innocence, but the songs do so without sentimentalising the imagined past. The world of rivers, gardens, railway lines, particular avenues, can be identified with Morrison's youth in east Belfast. The site of that past becomes emblematic, rather than turned into local colour. Indeed, throughout *Astral Weeks*, as with Morrison's later albums, the naming of streets, districts, regions, takes on incantatory significance. The memory returns again and again to its first home as the alluring poetics of space, rather than the specific meaning of the place.

Astral Weeks is not the sudden breakthrough of which it has so often been described; Morrison was after all working on these, and similar songs in Belfast well before leaving for New York. More importantly, the main thrust of the songs remains close in theme and imagery to his earliest recorded work with Them: tracks such as 'Hey Girl', 'Philosophy' and particularly 'Friday's Child'. There is too the clear line that runs through his first recordings with Bert Berns for Bang Records, such as 'Joe Harper Saturday Morning' and 'The Back Room'.

The significant shift is in the musical treatment. It has moved away from the hard-edged, probing 'group' sound with which Them channelled, indeed challenged, Morrison's voice. Instead the voice is articulated alongside the softer-focused, accoutisically-led accompaniment. For the guitar (Jay Berliner), bass (Richard Davis), flute (John Payne), vibraphone (Warren Smith) and drumming of the

Modern Jazz Quartet's Connie Kay fuse into an orchestration of strings. What is produced is one continuous mood-poem. Morrison's guitar might introduce the songs of *Astral Weeks*, but the poetic intention in his controlling voice is clear from the very beginning of the title track, 'Astral Weeks':

> To be born again, to be born again,
> To be born again, in another world darlin'
> In another world.
> In another time.

The desire in the voice, a hymn to love's possibility, picked out by the light touches of flute, strings and guitar, is guarded throughout *Astral Weeks* by a darker bass note that reminds us of uncertainty and vulnerability:

> Ain't nothin' but a stranger in this world,
> I'm nothin' but a stranger in this world,
> I got a home on high,
> In another land so far away, so far away.

Before Morrison laughs at himself at the song's end.

The setting for *Astral Weeks* could not be simpler: two lovers, separated 'from the far side of the ocean', are joined together throughout these love songs. They walk through gardens and experience one another in a dream state. (An earlier, less coherent version of 'Beside You' depicts their encounter in explicitly physical terms, with the male figure dramatised in a much more forceful sense.)

While this untroubled world seems out of reach, the songs record the poet's own surroundings, with intriguing and sometimes obscure references:

> Little Jimmy's gone way out of the back street,
> Out of the window, to the fog and rain,
> Right on time, right on time.
> That's why Broken Arrow waved his finger down the road
> So dark and narrow,
> In the evening just before the Sunday six-bells chime,
> Six-bells-chime,
> And all the dogs are barking.

The city landscape is left behind as 'the country where the hillside mountains glide' comes into view and in this Chagall-like transfiguration, the two young lovers meet, 'in the silence easy':

> You turn around, you turn around, you turn around,
> You turn around, and I'm beside you, beside you.

These love songs are all about an uncomplicated joy and the sense of release that singing his love's praises brings, troubadour fashion, as in 'Sweet Thing':

> And I will raise my hand up into the night time sky,
> And count the stars that's shining in your eye,
> Just to dig it all and not to wonder, that's just fine,
> And I'll be satisfied not to read between the lines.

The childlike love these songs court is literally of another time, even as the colloquial hints of 'read between the lines' bring a local feel to the song. In one of the best-known lyrics from *Astral Weeks*, 'Cyprus Avenue', Morrison re-imagines the play between young lovers:

> You came walkin' down, in the wind and rain, darlin',
> When you came walkin' down, the sun shone

through the trees
And nobody can stop me from loving you baby.

There is, though, a further element introduced in 'Cyprus Avenue' as Morrison touches upon inarticulacy, that much-vaunted feature of Northern Irish cultural identity and one which Morrison has explored (and made sport of) in live performances. In this instance, though, the issue is romantic (almost illicit) love. The expressiveness fights against itself, notwithstanding the Presley quotation, and tells a story of how difficult it is to say things; to communicate powerful feelings:

And my tongue gets tied
Every, every, every time I try to speak
And my insides shake just like a leaf on a tree.

What makes 'Cyprus Avenue' such an important song in Morrison's writing as a whole is the version of home which pervades it.

Is that 'Mansion on the Hill', Stormont—barely a stone's throw from the actual Cyprus Avenue? The railroad, that disused railroad which runs nearby Holywood, Bloomfield, Orangefield and Ballyhackamore? But what about those 'Six white horses on a carriage/Just returning from the Fair'? And what about that 'Yonder'—one of those words, which lives in northern vernacular, (as in 'Look at your man yonder') and with an archaic literariness. Indeed, 'Cyprus Avenue' reads like an old English lyric but sounds like a Belfast street-song. Between the formal poetry and the physical setting, Morrison's voice generates a troubled, robust ending amidst 'the avenue of trees'.

In 'Cyprus Avenue', and the other songs from *Astral Weeks*, an imaginatively coherent image of Belfast emerges, particularly of course for those who grew up in the city. As previously noted, the residential patterning of the parts of the city such as north and east Belfast revealed a scallop-shell of class segregation, not matched by other districts. Clustered around the lough on both shores, the working-class districts fanned out and upwards, via main arterial roads, spliced with boulevard avenues, and often embracing distinctive districts that had once been villages along with, in the 1950s and 60s, the new estates. The patterning incorporated rescheduled waterways, rivers, and streams as well as enclosing cemeteries, displaced big houses of once prosperous linen and shipping merchants, and maintained parks and green sites before reaching hillsides such as Castlereagh.

This red-bricked civic landscape of back lanes, 'entries', streets, terraces, roads and avenues had a definite if rarely articulated class formation. To move within it was to experience the all-too-visible distinctions of a provincial urban society. To move literally from it was to encounter the shifting magical thresholds between city and country. Morrison's songs are powerful testaments to both these levels of perception. The mysterious luminous quality of *Astral Weeks* is earthed in the wonder, surprise and customs associated with leaving his own back bedroom, going down his own street ('as we said goodbye at your front door', he says in 'The Way Young Lovers Do') to inhabit his own district, its daylight and nightlight, walking through Beersbridge and Orangefield, taking in everything.

Cyprus Avenue is not only a place, it is the idea of another place; the railway, the river: all are conduits through which Morrison's imagination is released.

'Madame George', the key lyric in *Astral Weeks*, dramatises this condition with a haunting portrait of belonging and leaving. This lyric, with its storytelling and repetitions, the anarchic mantra of 'the love' it seeks to express and its almost obsessive questioning, suggests comparison with the poet Patrick Kavanagh.

It is pure coincidence of course that Kavanagh, who was in the States in 1965 for a symposium on W.B. Yeats, should remark that he (Kavanagh) was all in favour of the Beat poets: 'I like Corso, Ferlinghetti, and Allen Ginsberg very much ... there are these lads in America, these youngsters that I admire very much.'

What Kavanagh saw in the work of the Beats is curious given the Irish situation he had in his mind. They had, he said, 'all written direct, personal statements, nothing involved, no, just statements about their position. That's all. They are not bores as far as I am concerned.' Kavanagh's voice of dissatisfaction with convention ('boredom'), strengthened by his subjective romanticism ('direct personal statements') is very close to the poetic vision of *Astral Weeks* and in particular to the voice which recites 'Madame George'.

I first heard the song early in 1969 from the US album somebody had obviously got a hold of and by the time it was released in the UK in September of that year, *Astral Weeks* had become cultic. Memory plays tricks with historical reality but it seems to me looking back to the twelve months between the end of 1969 and 1970, everyone was playing *Astral Weeks* throughout the Belfast which I knew.

That year was a watershed for every generation in Belfast but particularly so for those who were leaving their teenage years behind and becoming young men and women.

Friends would soon go their own way, across the water to England, taking up jobs, going to college, and disappearing. The months leading out of the 60s into the 70s correspond, loosely and in an inchoate and inarticulate way, with a social and cultural break-up of life as it had been known through the relative freedom of the preceding decade.

'Madame George' captured that feeling, and still does. It was a strange quiet before the storm. The clubs were still doing good trade; parties at weekends; visiting big names from Cream, Jimi Hendrix, Pink Floyd, The Small Faces played the Ulster, King's or Whitla Hall. People hung out and there was little 'aggro', except for the usual sort of fighting that made Belfast city-centre a dangerous place some Saturday nights. But you could walk throughout the wider city without too much anxiety or fear. Within a matter of a year or so, you took your life in your hands for so doing. 'At an age when self-importance would have been normal,' remarked Philip Larkin of the 40s, 'events cut us ruthlessly down to size.'

'Madame George' gives that freer time a distinctive sound and context. The shock of hearing the phrase, 'On a train from Dublin up to Sandy Row' has never quite left me. An inexplicable connection, coded beneath the words themselves, identified for the first time the actual city in which I lived.

Sandy Row, a Protestant working-class district in Belfast's inner-city through which the train runs, is named; the custom of throwing pennies into the Boyne River (the iconographic 'Protestant' site) which we did without knowing why, and the transfixing 'trance':

> Sitting on a sofa playing games of chance,

Astral Weeks (1968), a reverie of a lost Eden.

> With your folded arms in history books you glance,
> Into the eyes of Madame George.

Much has been read into this extraordinary song. For me, it is like an aisling, 'a child-like vision', which reveals a world of lost love, of ceremonies and evasions, past and present, shifting like a carousel between real and imagined people and places.

The soldier boy who is 'older now with hat on, drinking wine'—how many streets and roads had a few such veterans, tripping home after the pubs closed, at odds with the world they returned to after the war, and confounded by the front rooms, 'filled with music/Laughing music, dancing music' of a younger, more carefree generation?

'Madame George' is a portrait of a society about to withdraw from public view at the same time as the voice, which describes it, is also leaving the scene. Memories shift and coalesce. The site of the poem blurs and moves in and out of focus. It is the Belfast of Cyprus Avenue; there is a Fitzroy Avenue too. The rituals of 'collecting bottle-tops/Going for cigarettes and matches in the shops' are identifiably Belfast. But the journey is on a train from Dublin up to Sandy Row; and there is a Fitzroy Avenue in Dublin. Parsing the song in this fashion does not take us far.

What are constant are the voice and the connections that the accent makes between 'raps', 'cops', 'drops' and 'gots'. Quite simply, the song demonstrates what is truly unmistakable about Morrison's achievement—the steady, unflinching challenge which first his voice and then subsequently his lyrics and music embody.

The voice is a powerful ambiguity, revelling in itself, but dismissive too, while the lyrics explore (and corroborate) much of the imaginative ambition and desire of Morrison's poetic peers.

Astral Weeks, appeared the same year as Derek Mahon's first collection, *Night Crossing*. Clustered around that year too, one sees a new and powerful generation of Irish poets emerging out of the post-war period: Seamus Heaney, *Death of a Naturalist* (1966), *Door into the Dark* (1969); Michael Longley, *No Continuing City* (1969) with its 'Words for Jazz

Northern Poets: Michael Longley, Derek Mahon, John Hewitt, Seamus Heaney 1966.

Perhaps' updating Yeats; James Simmons, *Late But in Earnest* (1967) and *In the Wilderness* (1969); Stewart Parker, *The Casualty's Meditation* (1966), *Maw* (1968) (and whose 'High Pop' column in the *Irish Times* (1970-1976), hailed Morrison's albums with bright intelligence and insight). While from the south of Ireland, a poet emerged who probably shares quite a lot with Morrison in many respects, Paul Durcan, whose first publication, *Endsville* (1967), was co-authored with Brian Lynch, who subsequently wrote a stage play with the Morrison title, *Conquered in a Car-Seat*.

Like other Irish artists before him, Morrison's move to America was a liberating one at the time. The albums that followed *Astral Weeks*—*Moondance* (1970), *Tupelo Honey* (1971), *St. Dominic's Preview* (1972), *Hard Nose the Highway* (1973)—are an imagining of America and the extraordinary sense of freedom (as well as obsessiveness) associated with the place. As the literary critic and cultural commentator, John Wilson Foster has remarked about his own upbringing in east Belfast during the 1940s and early '50s: 'We grew up steeped in American popular culture. America was the fourth country we lived in.' It was all part of an extraordinarily potent mix. So the 'years of hope', that Jonathan Bardon described as the period 1945-1968, etched themselves eradicably in the emotional, cultural and political experience of an entire generation. Morrison gives voice to the hope and excitement, the energy and drive, shadowed by the knowledge of loss and pain. It is a curious coincidence that such a fusion is also at the core of another important east Belfast contemporary—the playwright, Stewart Parker, and particularly, in his greatest play, *Pentecost*.

In the mid-1960s Stewart Parker gave a special class at Orangefield on the poetry of Sylvia Plath. Afterwards, I spoke to him and confessed that I wrote poems. His smile was encouragement enough to a fifteen-year-old. Barely twenty years later, his untimely death at 47 in November 1988, robbed Irish literature of one of its most liberated and articulate voices.

When I saw *Catchpenny Twist* in the Peacock in 1977, the idea of Parker's liberating creative intelligence struck me, and again, with even more force, when I saw *Northern Star* in the Lyric in 1984. Field Day's production of *Pentecost* in Derry in 1987 showed Parker as a great playwright, and with Rough Magic's production of *Pentecost* (1995), this realisation came back with renewed conviction.

Pentecost is a contemporary classic, as central to Irish experience as *Translations*, *Double Cross*, *Bailegangaire*, and *Observe the Sons of Ulster Marching Towards the Somme*. Yet responses to the play point towards a kind of the cultural blind spot (to put it at its least contentious) when writing, bearing upon Northern Protestant experience, is addressed.

Pentecost takes place in east Belfast (Ballyhackamore) during the Ulster Workers' Strike against the Sunningdale Agreement between the British and Irish governments. The strike was in particular directed against the Council of Ireland dimension to that Agreement. The strike lasted from 14 to 29 May and was successful. It brought down the power-sharing Executive.

Pentecost begins in February 1974, moves into April, and focuses upon two weeks, from Sunday May 19, Saturday 25 through to June 2. Pentecost (Acts: 2) is a religious convocation marked in Christian churches on the 7th Sunday after Easter, Whit Sunday.

Belfast in 1974 was a ghost town; the workers' strike turned it fleetingly into a bizarre disconnected state-let. I was sitting my final exams that May and June and recall my stepfather driving me through roadblocks from east Belfast, stopping to get petrol at which the UDA guy in a balaclava, carrying a stick, flagged us on, and wished me good luck in the exams. '[T]housands of hooded men with clubs' as Parker has it in the play, but there was no widespread display of guns, contrary to conventional wisdom.

In the five years of the Troubles up to 1974, there were 1,000 dead, 620 of the victims in Belfast alone. Within the next year or so, 25,000 houses had been destroyed. In the first two weeks of May 1974, there had been 11 killings and 13 bombs had gone off. Sectarian warfare was engulfing Belfast: republican paramilitaries were destroying the civic life of the city with terrifying rigour. To go out and about, people literally took their lives in their hands. The loyalist response was nightly assassinations, bombing pubs and sacking streets. It is important to remember what the people of Belfast actually went through at this time—caught in a historical trap not of their making, their fate was to play out some undisclosable finale, defined and ultimately determined by the extremes of political demands.

As W.A. Maguire remarks in his study of *Belfast* (1993):

> ... in the first four years of the Troubles somewhere between 30,000 and 60,000 people in the Greater Belfast area were driven to leave their homes, at that date possibly the largest enforced movement of population in Europe since the Second World War.

Homes were burnt down; people were intimidated from their own houses and squatters moved in under the protection of one of the various defence committees. This is the backdrop to *Pentecost*. Hardly surprising, then, that Parker referred to the play being written in a form of 'heightened realism' and certainly not 'the conventions of a broadly realistic piece' by which it has been described. Parker makes his intentions clear in the stage directions: 'Everything is real except the proportions. The rooms are narrow, but the walls climb up and disappear into the shadows above the stage.' The atmosphere of the entire play, inhabited as it is with ghosts and ghostly figures of dead and haunted men, lost children, ominous shouts, scuffles, helicopter searchlights, jegs of broken bottles on the yard wall, drumming—these all create a claustrophobic world that is surreal.

Moving through the five acts are five characters: two Catholics—Lenny (to whom the house has been willed) and his estranged wife, Marian (who wants to buy the house); their two Protestant friends—an old college pal, Peter Irwin who has returned to Belfast from Birmingham, and Ruth McAlester, the evangelical friend of Marian.

The shade of the sitting tenant, Lily Mathews, custodian of Belfast history ('1900-1974. This house was her whole life,' Marian remarks) and in whose house the entire play takes place, enjoins a cast of unseen figures: Lily's own husband, Alfie, 'a good man'; Alan Ferris, the English airman and lodger, with whom Lily has had an all-too-brief affair, and a baby which she has given up, 'in the porch of a Baptist Church [to] ... moneyed people'; Ruth's demented RUC husband, who ends up in a mental asylum after repeatedly beating Ruth and turning upon himself; and the little baby of Marian and Lenny, Christopher, who lived for only five months.

The play is suffused with references to Protestant churches, Sunday school, hymns (Lily's singing of 'Rock of Ages' ironically corroborates the victory hymn of the Workers' Council); gospel (Lenny playing 'Just a Closer Walk With Thee'); mythologised northern Protestant experience of the First World War, the shipyard, the landscape and street names of east Belfast (Lily refers to her lover buying her a dress in 'Price's Window', a famous store where Albertbridge Road met Castlereagh Street). There is also a depth-charged link, easily mislaid in hastily formulated interpretation, between the significance of the play's title and the reality-altering vision which pervades and ultimately transforms the characters' lives:

> MARIAN: ... Have you never considered that if one of us needs treatment it might be you?

LENNY: I never know how you do this, I start off trying to help you, and within ten minutes, I'm a villain, I'm a deviant, I'm the one in need of help, in the name of God just face reality!

MARIAN: Which reality did you have in mind?

LENNY: Your own, Marian, your own reality, you've been talking to yourself, you've been counting spoons, you've been babbling in tongues in the middle of the night! ... What are we *supposed* to think?

MARIAN: Don't think, Lenny. Don't think anything at all. Don't even try. It doesn't agree with you. Here's what we're doing. I'm staying here with my tongues—and you're going home with your trombone. That way we're all quits. Okay?

One of the most powerful elements in the play is the way that Parker dramatically assimilates the apocalyptic, biblical vision (the babbling of tongues as the presence of the Holy Spirit) into the psychology of pain and loss which characterises the lives on stage, particularly the women's lives. Parker has also convincingly conceived women characters such as Marian and Lily, and less centrally, Ruth. While their childlessness becomes a subdued focus in the play, the dramatic metaphor of 'the house' as home and refuge becomes both moral and mystical shelter, as 'good' means 'washed', spotless, without blame:

LILY: Four of yous now, in on me, tramping your filth all over my good floors.

Within the house, Marian discovers Lily's diary as if it were a testament; while the christening gown of Lily's child, trimmed with lace and ribbons, merges naturally with the ceremonial white robes of Whit; and even Peter's awful bag of muesli can be seen half-seriously as a token of first-fruits. Be that as it may, the theatrical symbolism of the house is everywhere in the language of these broken characters. For 'house' read 'home-place', which means Belfast, Peter's Lilliput; whatever tensions surface, they revolve around possession, of being 'at home'. Having fled violence in her own home, Ruth attacks Peter for losing touch with his own people:

> RUTH: You don't know what's been happening here. What the people have gone through. How could you? You got out.

The moral weight of 'You got out' doesn't get in the way of Ruth and Peter making love, but it hangs over the play, like an indictment. Leaving or staying, homesick or sick of home, taking over a place or being evicted from it, the seesawing of the arguments between Ruth and Peter, Marian and Lenny—and which also include the infamous Harold Wilson broadcast, denouncing the unionist reaction as 'sponging on Westminster and British democracy'—all are based inside Lily's parlour house, 'eloquent with the history of this city', as Marian describes it.

It is a history which is class-conscious too, as Marian points out to her disenchanted trombone-playing husband: 'Well away you and explain all that to your Uncle Phelim [a psychiatrist], if you can track him down in his underground bunker, it's somewhere up Fortwilliam way, isn't that right?'

The Catholic upper middle class retreated towards the upper reaches of the northern side of the city; previously such districts had been the reserve of predominantly wealthy Protestant and Jewish communities. What ensues in this exchange between Lenny and Marian shows the extent to which Lily's house earths the dramatic force of

Pentecost. Marian starts to sound like Lily, and, at the age of thirty-three, she is Lily's age when Lily was most alive. Addressing Lenny, Marian says:

> MARIAN: I'm seeing this through. That's all. On my own terms. For Jesus' sake just leave me in peace, the whole shower of you, I'm sick of your filth and mess and noise and bickering, in every last corner of the house, I've had enough ... You find a refuge, you find a task for your life, and then wholesale panic breaks out, and they all come crowding in the door, her [Ruth] and you [Lenny] and that trend-worshipping narcissist [Peter].
> LENNY: It's beside the point, you're in terrible danger, we've all got to get out of here. The last thing I ever intended or needed, me and you under the same roof, it was another one of his lame jokes (*Gesturing skywards*) okay, we move out, we go our separate ways to our respective families. I don't like to see you in the state you're in. You're just not fit to be left on your own.
> (MARIAN *slowly turns on him*)
> MARIAN: What are you getting at?
> LENNY: I'm talking about what's going on!
> MARIAN: Such as?
> LENNY: What have we been having this entire conversation about?
> MARIAN: You consider that I'm cracking up?
> LENNY: When did I say that?
> MARIAN: Not fit to be alone?
> LENNY: In this house, that's all!

The talk is all about the place, at-home-ness: 'in every last corner of the house', 'refuge', 'door', 'roof' etc. Throughout *Pentecost* the notion of belonging and of sustaining relationships with one another and to one place, ramifies with similar terms of reference. But it is no longer 'just' the house; it is with living and being; or to use that desperate old Cold War jargon, 'co-existing': man and woman, Protestant and Catholic, the living and the dead; past and present. The history of this possibility—of redemption, self-belief, and common bonds, of sharing—is clearly established in the third act of *Pentecost*. Peter and Lenny are talking in superficial, blunt male terms about Marian:

> LENNY: It's the state she's in ... totally obsessive, don't ask me what the story is ... some weird syndrome, you know how it is with women. I'm just thankful she's finally agreed to a divorce.
> PETER: Would it still be losing the kid, maybe?
> LENNY: That?—oh, she took that in her stride ... didn't she ... no problem. Anyhow. It's five years now.
> PETER: Can't be.
> LENNY: Near as dammit. August '69.
> PETER: A vintage month.

August 1969 remains the watershed in many northern minds, particularly for those in their late teens and twenties living in the city, jockeying back and forth to London, caught up in the music of the time. It was the symbolic breakpoint, because after that date the North entered the nightmare; beforehand, it felt like an Indian summer of endless parties and club land.

Pentecost is a hymn to the self-consciousness of that lost time. Written as part of a triptych of history plays in the mid-1980s when the cycle of violence seemed unbreakable, Parker found in *Pentecost* a form for exorcising what he called the playwright's 'gift or sentence' which is 'to function as a medium, half-hidden in the darkness, subject to possession by the ghosts of other voices, often truer than his own'.

What formed Parker's own voice is neatly summed up by himself in a bright and witty piece he wrote on James Joyce called 'Me & Jim'. Coincidentally, it is a list of priorities which neatly contextualises the themes of *Pentecost*:

> My own mind was framed by an urban neighbourhood, a working-class family struggle towards petit-bourgeois values, a recoil from home and church and country, an appetite for exile.

I may be deluding myself but the voice of Stewart Parker, which I hear, has a faint American inflection and the style of the man links him immediately with my own generation. As Robert Johnstone remarked in his *Honest Ulsterman* tribute, 'Playing for Ireland: Stewart Parker: 1941-1988', Parker 'was only a couple of years younger than Michael Longley or Seamus Heaney, but he seemed to belong to a later generation, whose style was more optimistic and playful'.

Throughout the years of the Troubles, the sanity and wit and guile of Parker's plays logged the dismay, devilment and anguish of a generation, which could not believe that what was taking place in its home was actually happening.

The belief and conviction that we were all one, irrespective of religion, if not of politics, was shattered. That sectarian violence and the lurid respect and support it received from so many, often-distant sources had become a sickening reality that was poisoning every hope and expectation.

Pentecost plays out this tragi-comedy with a series of stories that are neither ponderous nor self-serving. In the powerful, concluding moments of the play, Parker captures the crazy contradictory energy of his characters and the cultural world they know inside and out:

MARIAN: I'm clearing most of this out. Keeping just the basics. Fixing it up. What this house needs most is air and light.

And as they tell one another stories—Marian and Lily's night of passion; Lenny recalling seeing 'a gaggle of nuns, real nuns, stripping off' and swimming, 'experiencing their sex'; before Ruth reproves him for not understanding what 'Christianity' is about:

> RUTH: You don't even know what day it is now, the meaning of it.
> PETER: You tell them, Ruthie child. Pentecost Sunday.
> LENNY: So what?

What follows is an extraordinary moment in Irish theatre and probably one of the most misunderstood scenes as well. It has been called 'a cop out' and 'dramatically problematic' and clearly caused critical unease but the misunderstanding has probably got more to do with cultural difference than many in Ireland or Britain are willing to acknowledge.

As the stories interweave, Ruth and Peter recite between them, 'The day our Lord's apostles were inspired by the Holy Spirit', to which Marian responds by talking about Christopher, the child she has lost. The scene, in what Elmer Andrews has called Parker's 'self-conscious theatricality', runs a great risk of falling like O'Casey into pathos, but the energetic and disciplined performances of both Eileen Pollock (in the original Field Day production) and Eleanor Methven (in the Rough Magic production) maintained the religious rhetoric with a strict and passionate delivery:

> MARIAN: Personally, I want to live now. I want this house to live. We have committed sacrilege enough on life, in this

> place, in these times. We don't just owe it to ourselves, we owe it to our dead too ... our innocent dead. They're not our masters, they're only our creditors, for the life they never knew. We owe them at least that—the fullest life for which they could ever have hoped, we carry those ghosts within us, to betray those hopes is the real sin against the christ, and I for one cannot commit it one day longer.

I don't read the scene as 'a self-conscious break with naturalism'; because the play isn't conceived in terms of the usual conventions of naturalism.

This speech, and Ruth's opening her Bible and reading aloud of the second chapter of Acts, is a metaphorical resolution, completely in keeping with the 'heightened realism' of *Pentecost*. Critics are uncomfortable with the tone, but target the style instead. 'Thou hast made known to me the ways of life; thou shalt make me full of joy with thy countenance' leads into Lenny's playing a very slow and soulful version of 'Just a Closer Walk with Thee' before Ruth opens the window, echoing Marian's earlier comment about what the house 'needs most is air and light'. I cannot think of a finer tribute of commemoration than this.

The ethos of *Pentecost*, taking into account its fun and laughter, and the caustic wit that sparks off between the couples, challenges certain kinds of (almost) subconscious critical categories, in Ireland and Britain. While *Pentecost*, particularly through Peter, condemns the lack of political generosity within the 'so-called Protestants', yet the underlying picture defies easy notions of cultural stereotyping. The play takes Lily as its defining point of reference and dramatically explores the complexity, limitations and connectedness of Protestant culture within northern Irish society. It takes that society as culture, not

Stewart Parker, playwright 1941-1988.

solely as prejudice, and cuts against the grain of received wisdom with a deeply human portrait of a stratum of a society in crisis.

Parker was well aware of what he was doing and in the Introduction to his *Three Plays for Ireland* (1989) he remarked:

> The ancestral wraiths at my elbow are (amongst other things) Scots-Irish, Northern English, immigrant Huguenot ... in short the usual Belfast mongrel crew, who have contrived between them to entangle me in the whole subject for drama which is comprised of multiplying dualities: two islands (the 'British Isles'), two Irelands, two Ulsters, two men fighting over a field.

Many writers and critics of Irish writing have problems with this reality and ignore it. Indeed, its critical invisibility is worth noting. For instance, in that most impressive and sweeping historical survey on literature and drama in Ireland, Declan Kiberd's *Inventing Ireland: The Literature of the Modern Nation* (1995), Stewart Parker's name does not appear once, not even in a passing reference. Yet I cannot think offhand of another playwright who, in the space of roughly a decade between the mid-1970s to the late 1980s, offered more light specifically on the various historical Irelands which inhabit the island of Ireland.

Parker was nothing if not switched-on to the here-and-now, the present, whether that be in his dramatic writing such as the charade of *Catchpenny Twist*, the poignant insights of the television play *I'm a Dreamer, Montreal*, or in the three plays which he saw as forming one historical meditation, 'a common enterprise' as he called it, closing with *Pentecost*.

As Parker said in his John Malone Memorial Lecture, 'Dramatis Personae' (June 1986):

> New forms are needed, forms of inclusiveness. The drama constantly demands that we re-invent it, that we transform it with new ways of showing, to cater adequately to the unique plight in which we find ourselves. For those of us who find ourselves writing from within a life-experience of this place, at this time, the demands could not be more formidable or more momentous.

Forms of inclusiveness? There is still a long way to go in being able to live up to Stewart Parker's comment about *Pentecost* when he remarked, 'for my own generation, finally making its own scruffy way onto the stage of history and from thence into the future tense'. *Pentecost* is about the everyday experience of political change. The play also marks the beginnings of real cultural shifts and (ironically) the demise of political hegemony, at the very point when the Protestant working and farming classes exercised their self-confidence most forcefully in political action. Until that point in May-June 1974, Belfast was a unionist city and its cultural ethos was Protestant. It isn't that any longer. Thirty years of the Troubles reached, surprisingly enough, a stand-off between the two dominant political and religious groups. Yet the geopolitical fault lines of the city are drawn even tighter today than they where when I was growing up in the upper north side of the city. That side of town used to be distinguished as 'mixed'. Not only did Protestants and Catholics live side-by-side but also a significant Jewish minority and a varied community of sects and post-war refugees. The cultural diversity we hear so much about these days was a living, if unexpressed, reality in the late 50s and early 60s. It died in the cut and thrust of the early riots, and throughout the intimidation, bombing and assassination campaigns of the 70s and 80s. By the Nineties the landscape had literally changed and the living diversity destroyed or gone underground.

Without in any way wishing to minimise the irredeemably scarred lives of those who directly suffered, it's important to consider the net cultural impact of the Troubles in Belfast. The centre-less city (grossly abused by bombers and then crassly re-imagined by history-less architects) has become totally sectionalised; hollowed out into political spheres of influence and control, with some contested and ragged remaining interfaces. While the part of Belfast where I grew up was, to some extent, integrated and civic-minded, according to recent findings quoted by Madeline Leonard, there are now 'more peace lines ... located in North Belfast than in any other region in Northern Ireland and their number has increased since the first ceasefires were announced in 1994'. The majority of children, again according to Dr. Leonard, 'do not have *any* friends from the other religious community and a substantial number have never interacted socially outside their own religious grouping' (emphasis added). The contrast is stark indeed, and depressing. For that neighbourhood of working-class terraces, corner shops, entries and allotments, nestled in behind lower middle-class three-storied houses with small gardens, fronting the main roads, rising further out towards substantial upper middle-class villas, with grounds and gardens, has been undermined. Picture houses, churches, parks, bowling greens, family shops and the magical nooks and crannies, all fitted into some kind of a community living together and experiencing the intimacies of otherness. Not ideal, not idealised, but a living, complicated, gossipy, respectful and coherent community that could deal with itself and with private lives as well.

What I saw on a recent return was an ugly inversion of all that. Houses bricked-up; in one attractive triangle which I knew like the back of my hand, the once sturdy family homes converted willy-nilly into flats; front doors with steel girders; gardens full of crap. Houses which I recalled standing, if sombrely, in Sunday afternoon light, blinds drawn, the outside door opened to the vestibule, were now demolished, or dark and tawdry versions of their earlier selves. Faceless Iceland hangars, the cheap made-over facades of Quik Fix shops, pound shops; big windy soulless petrol stations, derelict 1960s buildings patrolled by invisible security companies; even a spur of a motorway cutting its way right through what had once been a vibrant built-up district. Those who had lived in the inner reaches of the city had clearly fled to the suburbs or left the city for good. What I saw was the physical (psychic?) impact of political failure, sectarian head counts; a failure inscribed in the actual fabric of the place. It is a lesson in itself when politics is driven by sectarian and not genuinely civic concerns. If such generalised pictures can ever really be believed, the fall-out has taken on something of the following shape. The west of the city became 'West Belfast', a city in itself; north Belfast became a twilight zone, a lethal no man's land into which you strayed at your peril; the east withdrew further into itself while districts such as upper Ormeau, Ravenhill and Rosemount in south Belfast attempted the impossible, to hold on to as much of the shared non-sectarian Belfast codes and knowledge as was possible. It was the Canton of Hope and it survived the dark times better than most parts of the city. It is now becoming a multi-ethnic magnet and a litmus test for the Belfast of today.

The compass of Belfast has been redefined and territorialised in a radical 'decentring' of the city as a living, common civic space. The class dimensions of all this are plain to see and it may well be that the at one-time historically mixed areas will resurface in the years ahead, relocated perhaps but acting as some kind of bridgehead between the divided communities. The gated apartment blocks settling along the Lagan might show a new way forward, at least for those wealthy enough to avail of the opportunity and lifestyle. While the reclaiming and upgrading by young couples of significant parts of the older housing stock, in, for instance, the Ormeau area, could create its own kind of dynamic of renewal, provided that some sort of permanence and buoyancy is in place. On the other hand, this may well be wish fulfilment. For it is not fanciful, going on what we already know, to imagine a situation in which Belfast, if current negative trends develop unchecked, will break up into culturally and/or ethnically separated entities. As the English playwright, David Edgar, remarked of contemporary Britain, there is a danger when 'a society narrows its self-definition to a point where substantial sections of its population are excluded ... it will end up becoming Balkanised'.

So what should be a city with a definable hub of coherent, inter-related expanding outlying neighbourhoods, turns into fragmented bits of mutually antagonistic and segregated 'ghettos'; a truly shocking indictment of the political imagination post-peace process, not to mention the highly financed structures for reconciliation.

Yet Belfast with its lough, hills and surrounding countryside remains rich in possibility. One need only think of the cultural mix upon which the city was built, its maritime, commercial and industrial history, its literary, scientific and engineering achievements worldwide, to realise that human potential. Irish, Scottish, English; refugees from here, there and everywhere; religious sects, racial minorities, all with their own customs, aspirations, prejudices, ideas, experiences, desires, language and self-understanding: all their own histories.

The main political and cultural problem facing twenty-first century Belfast is just how the city can accommodate and foster this diversity without ending up as the cultural equivalent of a bland, second hand modernity (such as one sees in some recent architectural redevelopment) or a sectarianism in new clothes. The violence of political and sectarian hatred has deprived the city of creating something special out of its past. It seems inconceivable to think that Belfast could remain stuck in an historical freeze-frame and languish as a beheaded capital city in a stateless limbo, one year green, and the next year orange, obsessed with an irretrievable past.

Bearing in mind that a city (any city) cannot be fixed in one final version of itself, there is a critical value to be had from thinking about the kinds of continuity and crisis which made Belfast what it is: a culturally mixed city with a very mixed cultural past. Perhaps more power should be invested into Belfast and its environs so that it becomes a major regional centre, alert to its actual physical location, an arrival point between two islands and their various diverse cultures. It might be a good start if some of these blurred images and issues of authority and cultural identity were addressed honestly and clarified at a political level. To reduce this condition into a symbolic battle over flags and emblems would be further testimony only of the failure of political will to *overcome* the sectarian divisions of previous centuries.

The Belfast that I grew up in had much to recommend it, not that I appreciated it at the time. I can remember one key factor, which emerged during the late 60s, just before the curtain fell. It was the fleeting growth of a renovated, energetic, non-sectarian generation which was moving into place, at ease with nationality (indeed promiscuously post modern in that regard, well before 'hybridity' became fashionable), critically engaged by literature, politics and world events and motivated by a sense of civil society, defiantly rejecting tribal allegiance as backward looking. It had no singular imaginative voice, no newspaper, no critical mass and it took no institutional form. It was critically invisible and remains a phantom. Under the weight of living through the appalling bombings and the disintegration of Belfast into localised fiefdoms under paramilitary control, this amorphous, cultural 'cement' shattered. The common civic culture, which underpinned much of Belfast, has simply eroded, like its industrial, architectural, technological and maritime past, into folk museums and heritage photography books.

The younger generation probably doesn't know so much about the shadow-lands of that political and cultural past life in Belfast. The nightlife and pub-life of the city is today indistinguishable from Bristol or Birmingham, or, for that matter, Dublin's custom-built Temple Bar. We all live, more or less, in the same postmodern heaven or haven.

In his wonderful memoir, 'A Country Boyhood in

Belfast', John Wilson Foster's idyll, considered against the background of the Troubles, might appear today as wishful thinking:

> When I was a boy I lived in four countries. I lived in Britain, which we called England because all our playthings were stamped 'Made in England' on their under parts. England was toy land and, at the same time, the rather stern parent from whom the toys aloofly came. Northern Ireland was not strictly a country but the place where I ran, quite literally, my heedless ways. Northern Ireland, let's say, I lived rather than lived in. In the beginning was Belfast, which in turn meant the streets of our little canton, named after Shakespearean characters whom we did not know, and so we pronounced them as we saw fit—Oberon Street, Titania Street, Glendower Street. Had we known them we might have nicknamed our canton as wits had named the Ormeau district of Palestine, Jerusalem, Cairo and Damascus streets 'The Holy Land'. But where we grew up was, in any case, "The Holy Land."

It may be necessary and timely to remind ourselves that this past, a very real past, was inextricably linked with the British imperial project. To deny that is to falsify the historical picture in the interests of a virtual reality; a political monoculture. Industrialisation was at the very core of the imperial project and Belfast was a main centre of that global ambition whose religious and cultural filters meshed with Empire, colossal forces (of industrialisation and the British empire) which no longer exist. Few options were made available or openly debated by the leadership of such unionist communities when change—economic, social and political— bore down relentlessly during and since the Thatcher decades. Nostalgia, in its virulent, triumphalist, as much as democratic form, was held on to as if to a life raft. It didn't work.

In sharp contrast, the shift towards a European self-consciousness that the Republic of Ireland managed during the 1970s and 80s, sits uneasily in Belfast precisely because of its historically intimate and highly-charged emotional ties with war-torn Britain of the 1940s and 50s. The identification of the economic benefits that flowed (and still in large measure flow) from the British connection should also be taken into account. The North, and Belfast in particular, might have missed out on the Celtic Tiger boom years, but since the mid 1990s Belfast has been catching up. What sustained the city (and also paradoxically left whole sections of the community vulnerable) is the thriving dependency culture. High rates of employment reliant upon the administration and public sector; generational unemployment; the outreach of health problems established as a way of life ('on the sick'), the emotional and moral ramifications of the victim mentality and its implications as regards local leadership and civic responsibility, have all had profound and long-lasting economic and social results. So the battle over flags and emblems reproduces at a superficial visible level deeper resonance, concerning the credo and iconography of the past. The countering aspects of northern nationalism, however, appear all the more appealing to the 'outside' world of, for instance, multi-cultural England and its present Labour administration. This renovated Northern nationalism clearly demonstrates to the attending media a comforting and easily identifiable cultural equation: Irish equals nationalist equals Gaelic, a unified, coherent island people. A fiction, of course, and a lasting one, in spite of all that has changed over the past two decades and more, but so unlike the endless internal rows, negativity, bickering and gracelessness associated with the fractious unionist voice, forever locked in an imperial past which the English left behind, with only the occasional nostalgic lapse. One need only point to the issue of language itself to see how the cultural weathervane has shifted.

From being an underground and repressed language in twentieth century Belfast, spoken Irish is now a dynamic and empowering mark of cultural identity for nationalists. The revival of Irish as a spoken language throughout nationalist Belfast is truly amazing. The consciousness that culture—both uppercase and lowercase—is important to everyday life is intense and discussed on the airwaves and newsprint media. But the intensity comes from 'identity' politics; not poetry. And the same is true for the fabricated 'Ulster Scots' project borne under the sign of the Good Friday Agreement and the political equation then in fashion of 'parity of esteem'.

But what of Belfast itself? It has existed as an imagined place, more as war zone than twilight, Celtic or otherwise. One person's stereotype is another's dead certainty. As we have seen, for generations Belfast was considered in various intellectual and artistic circles as anathema to the creative spirit. Live there and perish. The shocking, unflattering images of the city in Brian Moore's novels such as *The Feast of Lupercal* and *The Emperor of Ice Cream* see Belfast as a desperate place, thwarting human affection, self-confidence and hope; yet the city remained unquestionably the *key* defining site of Brian Moore's creative memory.

If Joyce's turn of the last century Dublin was a city of paralysis, mid-century Belfast was deadly—a cramped and dampening place, not unlike Muriel Spark's Edinburgh. To survive meant to leave and find out what the world was like. Moore's novels from the mid 1950s can be read as his quarrel with himself and the hometown that never let him alone. Not so much as a place but as an idea, Belfast in Moore's mind means a northern Catholic professional middle class upbringing which haunts and taunts his writing with its religious ceremony, cultural etiquette and historical self-consciousness. Throughout his writing life, Moore deconstructed that legacy of Catholic nationalist aspiration with a cool imaginative rigour and sophistication. The formal clarity of Moore's novels, the narrative compression, bright delivery of conversation, the rarity of his polished diction and the implicit moral dilemmas his novels dramatise, placed Moore at an intriguing angle to popular critical expectations about the nature and meaning of what an 'Irish Writer' is, or should be. Like his accent, Moore was hard to pin down, along with the suave stylishness and urban wit, all of which strike me as peculiarly Belfast.

Exile, lonely and all as it may well have been, was the making of Moore's writing. In an article published in 1974, Moore remembered leaving Belfast on a ship bound for Liverpool and a government job:

> [A] man sitting on a suitcase beside me took out a Baby Power and offered me a drink. 'Your first time across the water?' he said, 'Yes,' I said. 'What line of work are you in?' I didn't know just what I was going to do in this British government job. I had bluffed my way into it. All I knew was I was being sent abroad to some place my French would be useful. So when the man asked what line of work I was in, I began to live out my private lie. 'I'm a writer,' I said. 'Ship's writer?' he said. 'No, just a writer.' 'Would that be good wages?' 'I don't know,' I said. Perhaps that's the way a lot of people become writers. They don't like the role they're playing and writing seems a better one.

In the ego-driven, celebrity-charged world of contemporary culture, that disarmingly anxious self-consciousness 'Just a writer' has mostly gone along with the quick-witted retrieval of the last sentence, as the internationally recognised Moore looks back to the younger self voyaging out from Belfast. The sense of leaving and being uprooted is specific to Moore's own personal set of circumstances. But it carries historical reverberation even if the hundreds of thousands who currently fly in and out of Belfast's two airports carry a very different sort of baggage to that of the generation who left, during the mid 1940s to, say, the mid-1970s.

The earlier generation was following a pattern of emigration, which had become a feature of working- and middle-class life in Belfast. Attachment to the large UK-based post war industries, at craftsman or managerial level, often meant travelling with the job. When work was not plentiful, looking for a job generally meant leaving, while the economic reasons for so doing assumed a different kind of meaning as the Troubles took root in the 1970s. Many tens of thousands decided, if they could, to re-locate because of the extraordinary population shifts that were taking place as a result of the social unrest, or simply to find a 'normal' society in which to settle and rear a family. As we have seen, against the backdrop of the relative stability of Belfast in the 50s and 60s, the provincial capital experienced some degree of prosperity. The problem was, as we all know now, that the upswing in opportunities did not percolate sufficiently throughout the various social strata of Belfast's unemployed and lower-paid workers, and the confidence to accommodate different versions of Irish identity proved either skin-deep or withered on the vine.

The cultural straitjacket seems all the more rigid if few of the economic benefits are widely shared. This experience of exclusion unquestionably fuelled the sense of grievance significant sections of the Catholic community felt at the denial of its legitimate political and cultural aspirations. Yet leaving was also a rite of passage, for Catholics as much as for Protestants who wanted to experience the wider, freer world beyond Belfast Lough. By the mid 1970s the matter had become rather more urgent, a choice in some instances between life and death, or between reliving the past and creating a different and possibly better future elsewhere. (In the last ten years or so the converse is true, as immigrants seek a future in Ireland.) Precious wonder then that the very fragility of self which Brian Moore's greatest novels embody is predicated upon the city, which he left. For Moore's characters possess a self-awareness unquestionably honed in the Belfast in which he grew up, such as how the individual deals with inordinate family pressures to conform to certain handed-down religious or political beliefs and conventions. *The Emperor of Ice Cream* is as much an examination of this moral condition in the explicitly Irish setting of Belfast as *The Statement* (1996) is in an implicitly European context.

And unlike many of his southern contemporaries, Moore seems uninhibited when it comes to exploring the sexual life, the passionate life of his characters, men as well as women. This might have some relation to the frank, almost defiant sexuality of Belfast city life in the 1940s—from the jubilant liberating influence of the massive US Army presence to the reaction against the socially conservative and puritanical ethos of the City fathers. Moore's characters developed into sexual beings, aware of the pleasure of the body but also keenly aware of the cost of their own solitariness when rejected by, or taking an irreversible step beyond, the inherited bonds of family and home. In the intense and vigilant upbringing of his own middle class education, Moore could not help but know how fraught the struggle was for self understanding when any hint of licence or criticism could be interpreted as transgression (letting down one's own 'side'); a kind of moral betrayal. The cultural configuration of such an inheritance can be viewed as distinctly Belfast-made.

So too in the opening canto of *The Rough Field* from Moore's northern contemporary, John Montague, Belfast broods as an imposingly dangerous and dark city:

> Catching a bus at Victoria station,
> Symbol of Belfast in its iron bleakness.

The 'iron bleakness' shuts out all possible light, although thinking back to a novel such as Sam Hanna Bell's *The Hollow Ball*, a different kind of sensual light radiates throughout the seemingly anti-sexual city where, to quote Montague's poem again, 'constraint is all' .

It is the case, however, that from eighteenth-century travellers to nineteenth-century politicians to twentieth-century writers, Belfast is bound to change in the mind's eye. Take at random examples from Patricia Craig's marvellous, *The Belfast Anthology* (1999). Seeds of disaffection are recorded as well as the intimate, incoherent reasons to love the place. Here is travel writer Paul Theroux's righteous dismissal of the city in 1983.

> I had never imagined Europe could look so threadbare—

such empty trains, such blackened buildings, such recent ruins: DANGEROUS BUILDINGS—KEEP CLEAR. And bellicose religion and dirt, and poverty, and narrow-mindedness, and sneaky defiance, trickery, and murder, and little brick terraces, and drink shops, and empty stores, and barricades, and boarded windows, and starved dogs, and dirty-faced children—it looked like the past in an old picture.

Twenty years earlier, in 1962, Kate O'Brien's response is significantly deeper, even if she miscues the future—a not uncommon feature of the 60s:

> Belfast is not hard. It is not a city of brisk here-and-now: it is not spruce and forward looking; it does not roar and rush night and day towards the 1970s, the 1980s. On the contrary, its pace is easy, and it trails its immediate past and Victorian haphazardy almost too indulgently. Walking the streets alone, especially at evening, I have experienced a sharp, unlooked-for melancholy, and an inexplicable sympathy with the untidy streets and people!

Belfast, more than many other European cities, has been stereotyped to death; its complex history in permafrost; its geo-cultural life as a port, haven, hellhole, spectacle, dumbed down before the term was invented.

Twenty years earlier again than Kate O'Brien's observation, the normally astute Sean O'Faolain doesn't mince words in *An Irish Journey* (1940) when he comments upon the ruthlessness 'with which the whole general rash of this stinking city was permitted to spread along the waters of the Lough'. He continues:

> All the hates that blot the name of Ulster are geminated here. And what else could be germinated here but the

revenges of the heart against its own brutalisation ... There is no aristocracy—no culture—no grace—no leisure worthy of the name. It all boils down to mixed grills, double whiskies, dividends, movies, and these strolling, homeless, hate-driven poor.

Caroline Blackwood's hauteur in 1973 has a similar snobbish, old-fashioned edge: 'And day after day-post-war, just as they were pre-war—in the wealthy suburbs of Belfast the wives of the industrialists went on reading the Bible, drinking sherry and eating scones.' Although, according to C.E.B. Brett in 1978, many were also having the time of their lives: 'Below the grimy and conventional surface, [Belfast] was a city bursting with a stimulating life of its own, fed by the conflicts hidden not far below the surface ... I still think that in the 1950s and 60s life in Belfast was probably more invigorating and rewarding than in Dublin, Glasgow, or any other provincial city of the British Isles.' A life which in many ways provides the subtext for the early novels of the Belfast writer Glenn Patterson, such as *Burning Your Own*, *Fat Lad* and *The International*, which take up where the fiction of Sam Hanna Bell left off.

In a letter to John Boyd, Stewart Parker catches the contradictory pull when, musing on Brett's *Buldings of Belfast*, he remarks, 'Maybe people will begin to realise that there is more to the place than ugliness and bigotry—that you can love it and hate it with the same degree of intensity.' A point which Patricia Craig expands upon in her introduction to *The Belfast Anthology*: 'From the current policy of decimation, sweep away the whole architectural heritage of Belfast, and stick up replacements as repellent as you can make them' down to 'all kinds of enduring indigenous graces, from the city's mountainy backdrop to a special kind of urban élan, along with psychic inheritances both salutary and oppressive', you will see that Belfast is not just about 'loss' and negativity'.

An interesting comparison comes to mind. Spanning the life of the old state of Northern Ireland, the poet Padraic Fiacc was born in 1924; heralding the new dispensation, Ciaran Carson was born in 1948. Both Belfast poets have imaginatively inhabited parts of the city with a truly shocking intensity that might be linked to the fact that, as Catholics, the city never quite allowed itself to be considered 'theirs' in the first place. Put at its crudest, in their work an appropriation of the city takes place that is simply not matched, or indeed attempted, by writers who come from a 'Protestant' background such as John Hewitt, Michael Longley, Derek Mahon or Stewart Parker. 'Catholic' writers such as Padraic Fiacc or Ciaran Carson absorb everything, from the grim and ghastly to the glorious, with glee and devotion.

Whatever goes on it is a powerful imaginative ambition that we make contact with in Carson; in Fiacc, we find estranging, shocking menace. The bits and pieces of Belfast, which Carson has monumentalised into song, sonnet and fiction, are locally charged historical readings of place-names, streetscapes. He is like a traditional bard singing the praises and problems of his own people and their town land; it just happens to be a city, called Belfast. Carson fell in love with Belfast's past and has turned its dead industrial life into a vibrant figment of his own imagination. No other writer has achieved such redemptive fidelity.

On the other hand, Fiacc, from the Markets, is the last living embodiment of the spirit of the Celtic Twilight, passed to him by Padraic Colum in New York in the 1940s, where Fiacc lived the life of an expatriate Belfast man. Profoundly Catholic, and as politically incorrect as it's possible to be, Fiacc is without doubt the greatest untold story of Irish writing. The last of the last modernists, and a name to conjure with, he is now secluded in his room in a retirement home in south Belfast. Fiacc's shocking travails, however, of broken-down collapse and self-mockery, are a bitter journey to the twentieth century underworld, and the tragi-comic past of the city he has lived in, off and on, for most of his eighty-odd years.

It may be coincidental that one of the poems from Ciaran Carson's *The Irish for No* (1987) which took him into a new verbal and imaginative territory should be called 'Belfast Confetti'—'Suddenly as the riot squad moved in, it was raining/ exclamation marks,/Nuts, bolts, nails, car-keys'!— a phrase wryly conjured up by Fiacc in his earlier, 'The British Connection', from *Odour of Blood* (1973):

> And youths with real bows and arrows
> And coppers and marbles good as bullets
> And old time thrupenny bits and stones
> Screws, bolts, nuts, (Belfast confetti).

(*Belfast Confetti* would also become the title of Carson's subsequent volume published in 1989.) The anti-poetic of Fiacc's verse challenges the syntax and harmonic of 'Irish poetry' and mocks the very (Yeatsian) notion of poetry as a 'certain good'. The high oratorical ('Irish') literary past is killed off with lethal Belfast black humour. In Carson's poetry the names of things (literally anything) become the key. Is this nostalgia for the real thing? Names map the past like ruins that haunt our present. Carson's poems strain energetically, self-mockingly for authenticity, new points of departure between the past and present, the here and now, as he sees other cultures through the sights and sounds of his native city. The significance of Fiacc and Carson, Patterson and others whom I haven't mentioned here, is a powerful 'local' statement of a global condition.

Once a key to the industrialisation of the late nineteenth to mid-twentieth centuries, Belfast is now the imagined site upon which the end of these issues plays out. The city sits looking all ways at the same time, not unlike the mighty shipbuilding gantries of Samson and Goliath that straddle its sky, the dramatic remains of a past civilisation, like the very Titanic itself. So be it. Whoever said ways of life would last forever? The artistic restoration of the brave Albert Clock symbolically points the way for a true renovation of Belfast's physical and cultural landscape. The 'unique Irish city of Belfast in the great international cultural project of modernity', that John Wilson Foster evokes in his *The Titanic Complex*, is now something else. What that may be is another day's work.

II

BIT PARTS

for T.Q.

'The woven figure cannot undo its thread.'
—Louis MacNeice

I

MY GREAT GRANDFATHER WAS AN Orangeman. The story goes that there would have been a banner dedicated to him but his family demurred. I never met William. He was of Huguenot stock, married a woman of another refugee stock and fitted into Belfast life as a man of his turn-of-the-century times. I was fascinated by him, growing up in north Belfast in the late 50s and early 60s. His name was still known around and about and that intrigued me as mementoes of his life were still kept in the house, particularly one that I have to this day. It is a newspaper cartoon, which shows him, a pair of britches in hand, an old-fashioned, unadorned sash over his shoulder, tearing across cobblestones under the slogan, DUTY CALLS! When I was a kid I hadn't a clue what that duty meant and it was just as well that William was well gone because we would have rowed the bit out over his patriarchal unionism.

'Duty Calls', cartoon of William Bailey Chartres.

Throughout the late 1950s I was taken to watch the Twelfth of July parades. We would stand outside the City Hall, our backs up against the ropes, and wait for the carriages to arrive, within which the grandees of the different Orders stood and there would be a kind of embarrassed banter as the Preacher, with his doomful black sandwich-board Proverb strapped to his chest, raising his heavy Bible up in the air and stamping his foot, called vengeance or foreboding upon us all. Were we sinners?

Behind, the kiss-me-quick-hat brigade linked arms and danced; jolly little women with Union Jack skirts, aprons and bowler hats, like butchers, waved umbrellas, and the bands streamed by, wedged between them, serried ranks of men, waving, pointing their sons towards mothers, wives, brothers with infants on their shoulders, and the music cascaded down Royal Avenue and veered right and left again and on down the Dublin Road. 'Kilty' bands, military bands, flute bands, bands from Scotland which were called hucky-mucky, men with shining white gloves, sabres, little trays with icons placed on them, banners of all marvellous silks with images of queens, kings, stern men, martial figures, historical settings; and sometimes there would be a delay in the procession, and a band would stop in front of you and you could watch the bandsmen and their leader walking around them and the banners would sway some more and the young boys who held the black or white or orange strings would twirl them in their hands, or the big drummer would have someone hitch up the drum for a brief rest, although I never saw then a lambeg drum; never in all my life.

We did not go to the Field. Sometimes we'd return after tea to see the men come back though. But by the mid-60s that had stopped. Something was creeping in which seemed different from before. Then we stopped going altogether. I don't know why. All I remember is the Eleventh Night and the flames bursting up into the sky in the Brickies behind our home; and in the morning the drum-roll as a banner was unfurled in the Grandmaster's back garden in a house I could see from my back window. Tea was served and then the lodge joined up with its band and they made their way along Jellicoe Avenue and Alexandra Park onto the Antrim Road towards Clifton Street and the beginning of the Belfast procession.

Many years later, when all this ceremony was known worldwide as standing for only one thing, a triumphalist bazaar, I wrote a sequence of very short poems about growing up in north Belfast called simply, 'Six Scenes':

> The Past Master's
> taut face gleams
> like the window
> of his makeshift
> glasshouse.
> The teacup shakes
> from stiff gloves
> he has on as
> the banner unfurls
> to a swaying scene
> of Slave and Queen.

It would take a great film director like Antonioni to capture the unbelievable clash of pomp, propriety, machismo, bigotry and pride that went into those Twelfth celebrations in the '50s and early '60s. They were street-theatre before the term was invented; like Corpus Christi, without Christ.

II

In the 1950s, London was our second home. Half our family had emigrated to the English capital early on in the century and there was a regular jockeying back and forth from London where my great aunt and her extended family lived. We travelled by boat and train and eventually by air. We attended weddings and funerals, holidayed there, and I lived there for a little while before opting for Belfast in the late 1960s.

As Belfast Protestants, not of the churchy or party-political type, Britain existed as England. It was the cyclorama to our lives. We listened to the BBC on the radio, and watched BBC and ITV when the time came. Our house retained the blackout blinds from World War II up to the late 1950s. The bottled sauces and Indian tea, Camp coffee and medicines, brand named jumpers and socks, Tate & Lyle Golden Syrup with its sleeping lion and sleepier slogan, Christmas cake and boxes of biscuits were all British Made; my toys, too, and comics and footballs.

When it came to school, our history was British and the songs (along with accompanying gestures), which the slightly electric Miss Gray taught us, were English and Scottish ballads:

> My body lies over the ocean
> My body lies over the sea
> My body lies over the ocean
> O bring back my body to me.

The fact that it was *bonnie* seems to have passed us by. And the headmaster of my primary school, the mythopoetically named Mr Nelson, reputed to have looked

163 Duncairn Gardens, maternal family home, North Belfast, now demolished.

exactly the same when my uncle attended, a generation earlier, walked about with a raffish stoop and had, in his small unlit office, two memorable symbols—a fighter-plane on a Perspex mantle and a globe of the world demarcating the Empire. He was a proud, dignified and tolerant man, so far as we could tell, and he never interfered in our lives. On the other hand, the teacher who looked like Clark Gable, spoke with a distinct twang under the voluptuous moustache, and smoked Senior Service, bore all the marks of a devil-may-care veteran. The War was the centrepiece in our upbringing. Its effect on the Belfast of my boyhood was clear. Behind our house, the Brickies—a derelict site; above us, the deserted US Army installation—a warren of outhouses and garages; away below us, prefabs which housed hundreds of families whose homes had been destroyed when Belfast was blitzed in 1941.

And the stories of my great grandmother sitting through the Blitz under the stairs, giving out to the Jerries as an unexploded bomb lodged in the back wall; my grandmother working in a munitions factory, ducking IRA bullets; my mother's romance with a touring Army bandsman, and the men you could see and hear throughout the 50s and 60s, on the buses late at night, or stumbling home of an evening, regimental blazers and grey flannels, talking away to themselves or to their indignant yet knowing wives.

III

Football was with me from a very early age. My great-grandfather had been one of the founders of the Junior League in Ireland and he had earned his crust as a young reporter sending in reports from matches from far-flung reaches of the province. When I was very small, my father took me to Solitude, the Cliftonville ground, home to the Reds, amateurs as they were then in the early 1950s. A little later, when we moved to Skegoneill, my bedroom overlooked Brantwood, a small pitch that figured large in our lives. It had a spooky deserted house on one flank, the southern bank of the ground was sufficiently raised so that you could look down over lower north Belfast, and way beyond, and the sweeping pleasure-lands of The Grove, where I spent most of my boyhood evenings, ran to its easterly walls. A friend was the mascot of Brantwood as a result of which we attended the entire home 'fixtures' with semi-official status.

I played left back, and occasionally the slightly more glamorous left half, for primary school and boy scouts but didn't really make the grade in the highly charged devotion to 'soccer' at secondary school. By then I had switched allegiance and attended Seaview on the Shore Road, the gallant home stadium of The Hatchetmen, Crusaders, nestling along the foreshore of the lough and the North Eastern Railway:

> Bimbo Weatherup
> hammers one in;
> the crowd goes daft;
> a train shoots past.
> On the hill
> in front of us
> the houses stretch up
> like a ladder from
> the Shore to Antrim Road.
> In-between is where we are,
> backs to the sea.

Linfield, or the Blues, the pan-Belfast club based at Windsor, had a ferocious reputation and when they travelled to the Shore Road there was a sense of an army on the move. Crossing town every day to school on the east side brought me into the 'Glens' territory (Glentoran) and the swinging army-surplus satchels of Glens-obsessed supporters. Those were passionate times in which the slightly Anglo-fied voice of Captain Danny Blanchflower, ('ore play-eers') cut a dignified swathe through the fucking and blinding that went on back home in the swaying terraces of men and boys. The white immaculate v-neck of his Tottenham jersey said it all: he was our better half; our white knight. It was Derek ('Deek') Duggan (Wolves), a towering unconquerable one-of-the-lads, behind whose shadow would wistfully and shyly emerge the artist in us all, George Best. When Kenneth Wolstenholme spoke his name on 'Match of the Day' on Saturday nights, Best had become a real star, a shooting star.

The Belfast of the 50s and early 60s was for me synonymous with football. Whatever psychic clock we worked to, changing games by season without any announcement or instruction, from conkers, 'marlies' and a particularly painful hand-game using lollipop-sticks, to street games whose names I cannot recall, football was the air we breathed.

Hallways, monk's benches full of boots, yards, entries, back gardens, parks, side streets, pitches, jerseys, bedrooms bedecked with posters of teams and star players (alongside the motorbikes and the few 'rock' bands), imitation league-tables, flags, pendants, arms tattooed with 'transfers', schoolbags scrawled on, summers totally given over to talking and playing football, picking a team (and the gaminess and machismo of that) until night fell and you couldn't even see the ball. A famous newspaper competition was called 'Spot the Ball'—an act of pure imagination, if ever there were one. And the ball itself, a sodden heavy laced leather ball, a 'bladder', until the new plastic football came in and the machinery that went with keeping it inflated and the constant jockeying to and from the local shop, Billy Duddy's, to get the new footballs or better ones. And the reluctance to give this all up come September and the return to school when the professional season returned in England and the local versions that ran from the top clubs to the rest around us, like Brantwood or Chimney Corner and that ticker-tape on BBC Grandstand before the voice (what was his name?) gave the full results throughout the English and Scottish league tables: Steinhousemuir; Plymouth Argyll; such names with which to conjure on a dark Saturday night in the middle of February.

> The baize tablecloth is velvety with age,
> the tassels torn. You stretch on a sofa
> watching Tottenham Hotspur walk
>   all over Sheffield Wednesday.
> Whitewash on the backyard peels in scales
> and the slack weeps in its makeshift shed.
> The rain drip-drops down gutters and drains.
> Let there be another Ice Age, a God to speak with Moses,
> the skies open up and rivers part—
> this is where a young man finds himself,
> at half-time making tea by the sink,
> below glass-panelled presses that give back a look
> of the great-grandfather on his mother's side.

By the mid 60s all of this had given way to music although the World Cup flared up like a spectacular piece of theatre but the intensity had gone, along with the kind of life of that time.

Years later I was back outside our old house recording a programme for local television about leaving and crossing borders. I suggested we go into the football ground that I used to look into from my bedroom window and beyond it towards the amber city lights of Belfast. As we approached, the crew and myself, the door opened and one of the groundsmen stepped out. Behind him, tethered on a rope, and totally unenamoured by our presence stood a ram, his jagged horns twisting this way and that and those shocking eyes. It was a bizarre, almost perverse image out of the classical world—as if we had trespassed upon some hallowed ground of the past and that this detached, self-preoccupied custodial creature was there as a rebuke. 'Hey, mister', one of the goat's minders shouted, 'would you take our photee?' I bate a hasty retreat from the low walls, the hut of changing rooms, the slagging and counter-charges as men shouted at referees and each other; the straight-backed, Gladstone-collared Club president, the summer carnival that set up shop every year, the kick and rush and smash as the bladder thudded into the top of the net and the two or three young lads peering through the dusk into the haunted house when the match ended.

IV

Like thousands of other Belfast families Bangor to us represented the summer. It was to Bangor during the 50s that we went for a holiday, renting a house wherein my mother, sister and grandmother lived and which several of their friends visited from time to time. Occasionally my uncle and his pal dropped by but outside of some time spent on the Ballyholme beach, their minds were fixed on the bars and dancehalls.

A taxi took us to the Northern Eastern station. The train journey from Belfast to Bangor was a ceremonial affair of expectation that was only ever complete by entering the station in Bangor, stepping into the main street and looking down towards the clock tower, the Mine and the rattling chains of coal buckets or the spinning wheel of the little Fair.

We stayed in comfortable red-brick houses with tidy gardens and small backyards. The houses were full of heavy furniture and indistinct carpets, stairways and cubbyholes, shadowy back bedrooms and craft-worked etchings of the Mourne Mountains, Helen's Bay or some well-known 'place of interest' like the Mull of Kintyre or Portpatrick. The few books around were miscellanies; Saturday Bedside anthologies. Firescreens and tables of one sort or another covered the hearths or popped up out of corners, at bay windows, between doors.

We had connections in Bangor, friends of my grandmother's. One had a shop in the main street and we visited for tea, enviously eyeing their son, a tanned and athletic young man who worked his summers on the pleasure boats. Another friend of my grandmother's, who intrigued me with her quiet manner and distinctly 'country' accent, lived in Prospect Road and had fostered our dog when we moved house from suburban Belfast to one of the busy arterial roads on the city's northside. She and her sister passed 'snaps' of men and women I knew nothing about between them and smiled a lot. We went from their house into Ward Park to look at the big Gun, flowerbeds, and Bowling Green and then took in the last of the evening sun. There was something 'hurt' about the sisters.

From time to time my grandmother's Belfast friends breezed in on day visits or even stayed a night or two by way of offering her diversion. Their 'real' holidays were spent in Douglas, Dublin or Bournemouth and she also visited her sister in London. I fell in love with one of those friends at the age of six or seven. She had flaming red hair and adoring eyes and smoked 'plain' cigarettes, the lipsticked stubs of which she left like love tokens in ashtrays around the place.

On deckchairs we would sit facing the sea. The ice cream shop on the promenade was like a little bunker and up above it stood tall silent guest houses. Most afternoons beyond Pickie Pool, and throughout Sundays, songs were sung and although we never took part, we would listen and move on.

> Each little flower that opens,
> Each little bird that sings,
> He made their glowing colours,
> He made their tiny wings:
>
> The purple-headed mountain,
> The river running by,
> The sunset and the morning,
> That brightens up the sky.
> —Mrs. C. F. Alexander: 1823-1895

I couldn't swim then but jumped about at the water's edge, took a net to the rock pools or ventured towards the diving rafts marooned when the tide went out. It was a regular life of simple enough pleasures and expectations.

I don't know what we talked about nor can I recall either a television or radio being about the place. The good air was what we were there for and doing nothing else save for the life on the strand, walks and preparations—for endless salads, sandwiches and tea. I'm not even sure that we went to the Fair or the evening entertainments which must have been available, such as shows in the Town Hall, or the cinema.

Everything seems to have had a rhythm of its own: a steady, enclosed unselfconscious flow. What the adults talked about when we were in bed—health, family problems, the news of the day—all that was as remote as Belfast itself. Bangor was for that time another life, suspended in time. The boathouse, the rocky shoreline, the tree filled headland, the lights on the far side of the lough, the ships and tankers moving slowly in and out of Belfast's invisible docks, the bustle of men, women and children strolling down the promenades or sitting on the walls, kids playing 'tig' on the beaches, and the unimpressed demeanour of the private villas and gardens, halls and churches, made it all appear so secure and present for all time. What individual lives were being led had no bearing since we were the visitors, the outsiders who no doubt toyed with the notion of moving there for good 'one day'. That comforting delusion ran aground by the time we packed up and took the train home again, subdued, reluctant and relieved.

Bangor became a different place for me in the mid to late 60s; that's another story. In the early 70s I returned once more—the last family trip, like a reunion you could say and, some years later, I wrote a couple of poems, including 'Responsibilities', as a kind of homage to the unexplored life I had known there, as a young boy, playing on the Down coast.

Responsibilities

> The child turns in a cot
> and stars increase what hold
> they have over the infirm
> and forgotten whose time
> this is, near enough to dawn,
> when back rooms are washed
> with light and down along
> the Esplanade the sea booms
> around the shining rocks.
>
> It's like I haunt this
> dormitory town of parks
> and one-way streets,
> of evangelical picnics
> and children screeching
> through days on the beach,
> for there in the rented
> redbrick holiday homes
> families keep the faith,
>
> and for all I know,
> those who lie awake
> reading the Old Testament
> dream of tomorrow's excursion
> and pray for the sun.

V

One morning in 1965 I was sitting on the 64 Downview Bus, heading into the city centre for school. It was raining and the bus was packed with people, most of whom were smoking cigarettes and looking out the steamed-up windows. A strange thing happened. I looked around me and in a flash of histrionic insight, realised, almost smugly, that, like the drunken Minister in the film *Zulu*, they would, we all would, someday die. No proverbs; no sandwich men; no ministers; no amount of praying, church-going or piety could get us around that simple fact of life.

A few years later, I read until I was almost blue in the face everything by Jean-Paul Sartre and Albert Camus and considered that my earlier experience had been what every good existentialist knows to be an encounter with the Absurd. If Roquentin, Meursault and Mathieu, leading figures in their fiction, were not exactly the best role-models for a Belfast Protestant teenager, with a paltry attendance at Sunday school and church, who was supposed to know any different?

The irony is, I suppose, that the family I came from, while not being orthodox in their religion—anything but—did have a lot of time for spiritualism. Life-after-death was a fairly acceptable norm. Not things that go bump in the night, hovering tables and trumpets of ectoplasm like a week's washing—although there was one book with photographs of such things that had a faintly Faustian sense of transgression about it, and still has to this day. No, the spiritual dimension to my upbringing ran quietly but constitutionally contrary to the eyeballing of existence upon which Sartre insisted. But, like a dutiful disciple, I was hooked by his militant agnosticism.

Roquentin remarks in *Nausea*—Penguin Modern Classics, June 1969, four shillings, Dali's 'Triangular Hour' on the cover:

> Most of the time, because of their failure to fasten on to words, my thoughts remain misty and nebulous. They

assume vague, amusing shapes and are then swallowed up. I promptly forget them.

And the rallying call I underlined clearly held no truck at all with religion, spirituality or the likes of that.

> I want no secrets, no spiritual condition, nothing ineffable; I am neither a virgin nor a priest, to play at having an inner life.

Why an 'inner life' should have been seen then as an almost derisory thing I cannot now recall. Yet, the thirty and more years which separate the underliner of that passage from the present writer has also seen, in Ireland as elsewhere, a great emphasis being put upon the public confession of one's innermost secrets and personal experience. The more beans of self spilled on stage, in print and on TV, the more honest, sincere, genuine, moving, powerful and realistic we are seen to be. In fact, confession has become not only a marketing tool but a lifestyle. A private life is not a life unless everything is exposed from the inside out.

In rejecting all this tosh, the Duchamp portrait by Jacques Villon on the Penguin cover of *The Outsider* says it all. Angular, haunting, and uncompromising, it embodies a feeling of calm, benign, hard-won indifference. Resisting sham solutions, self-indulgence, fashionable anger, privileged resentment and preoccupied instead with austere moderation and artistic reserve, it should come as no surprise that Camus offered an alternative, if allied, vision to that generally on offer in post-war, pre-Troubles Belfast.

It is something which Derek Mahon captures in his poem dedicated to Camus, 'Death and the Sun':

> The interior dialogue of flesh and stone,
> His life and death a work of art
> Conceived in the silence of the heart.

'Existentialism' was an aggressive way of bringing oneself up in a city coming down with religion and atrophied politics. It was a thing of the heart; iron in the soul.

> On everything I love, on the rust in the yards, on the rotten planks of the fence, a miserly, sensible light is falling, like the look you give, after a sleepless night, at the decisions you made enthusiastically the day before, at the pages you wrote straight off without a single correction.

What Roquentin writes in his diary was the real thing.

Where the spiritualism came in is something else—a joker in the pack, the hazel wand that bewitches and divines 'truth' rather than discerning 'the reality of a situation'. This belief in an afterlife had a strong, palpable existence in the north of my childhood, possibly as a throwback from the mourning of two world wars, I don't know.

But it is something without which the suffering in the north of Ireland would have been even more unbearable for the bereaved. The testimony during the Troubles of so many in front rooms talking of their murdered loved ones, bespeaks a faith in God, in an afterlife, that cannot be overlooked.

So, I am less sure about religion. It has staunched many wounds, ritualised and dignified what is so grim in its very ordinariness—death. If institutionalised religion lacked sunlight that probably tells us more about the north as a whole, than it does about its churches and those who go to them. As Mahon's poem says:

The modes of pain and pleasure,
These were the things to treasure
When times changed and your kind broke camp.

Times are changing. Rigor mortis, not rigour, is setting in with those who remain glumly satisfied with their own religious or political self-consciousness. But if pleasure comes from God, a church bench, a meeting hall, or a marquee tent, who is to decree: No, that's wrong? It is, isn't it, a matter for the individual and his or her own free will and conscience?

VI

It was a choice between Art History in England and English in Northern Ireland. Queen's in Belfast was too much like home and when a friend said he was going to (what was then called) the New University of Ulster, that was it. We headed off in his black Morris Minor one September morning in 1971 and moved into the same B&B for the first term. The house was run by a businesslike woman who took good care of us, and her house. Everything was in its place, put there with a kind of brisk love.

Going to university was not the logical thing to do. Most of my friends either had not bothered or did not get the chance. We were, after all, children of the '60s, full of grace, and it took some time to settle into the troubled world that the '70s brought. Anyway, Coleraine in 1971 was a compromise. The campus looked like an airport but, behind it, the Bann curved its way towards the coast and the magnificent sea—along the shoreline of which holiday resorts clung, full of three- and four-storied guest houses with great bay windows like puffed-out bellies—and a thin wind that would cut right through you.

It was not long before a few of us—mostly from Glasgow and Belfast—had banded together and joined the Labour Club. NUU's political birth had been uppermost in many minds but, accepting the fact it was there to stay, we sat in seminar rooms and discussed the 'Law of the Diminishing Returns of Profit' and held a radical stall outside the refectory every week. When things were looking bad, some of us formed the 'James Larkin Defence Committee' and planned to get threatened Catholics out of isolated places into safety. And we went on marches, to meetings and watched steadfastly as everything went from bad to worse. But we lived in a triangle that was symbolic in a way— between Coleraine, Portstewart and Portrush, the lines of communication were open and you could live freely, if experimentally, across the divides. Politics grew into Irish culture and back again into literature. We mixed into traditional music and some of the traditional musicians mixed into politics. I started to play in a band called 'Fir Uladh' and we performed at various venues, from anti-internment rallies to folk concerts. It was blissful. And, because I had written some poems, which were published and broadcast, the Irish Dramatic Society asked me for a play. I wrote one—a short incoherent thing, the idea of which I had lifted from Robin Flower's *The Irish Tradition*— and called it *The Skull*. It was duly translated into Irish and, travelling with it, I was proudly introduced once as 'Our Belfast Protestant' to a smiling group of anxious Dublin Gaelgóirs.

We shared a year or two of confusion, living within that

strange triangle. The people who lived there were mostly hospitable to these students in their midst. Even though our lifestyle was, on the face of it, a challenge to their own, I never heard a bad word said against us and only once in Coleraine did I hear 'the bigot' come out in a person. He was drunk and on his way home from the bar. The group of us, from all over the north, Scotland and England, and from every 'side', gazed at his ignorance and smiled sagely that his was an ugly old world shuffling off its mortal coil.

The three years did not last long. They were intense though. Everything was—sitting in the campus listening to the news of the Abercorn restaurant bomb blast, watching the slow dismantling of Belfast and the places we used to meet in back home. We threw darts in the university bar, while the literary critic and novelist Walter Allen held court, sipping pink gins and smoking his endless stream of untipped Senior Service cigarettes. Ensconced in the Anchor Bar, nestling beneath the convent in Portstewart, or in the Harbour Bar in Portrush, poet James Simmons' home from home, there was an air of unreality about the whole time and place.

The people of 'The Triangle', however, lived their lives with a keen knowledge we did not have. They were wise before the event and had an almost stoical single-mindedness about what was happening around them, as if it were a bad season they just had to thole. And us? The lectures went on as usual for those who cared to attend.

I remember, for instance, in one linguistics class, the distinguished professor, noted for his abstract convoluted manner and celestial gaze, talking us through the derivation of Cornish place-names. Three ex-Oxfordians sat midway up the lecture hall rigged-out as 'Red Indians' with war paint and headdresses as a bet to show how oblivious the lecturer was of what was going on before him, one of their cats mewling in the aisle.

Such frivolity disappeared with time. The atmosphere became more obsessive, nervous, and shaky. We held together, a generation at sea, but slowly being roped back in by the past. Some returned home to discover the police had lifted brothers, badly beaten, interned; or a man down the road was murdered, or another Provo bomb had scorched the life out of this street or that, and the inevitable retaliation. Every day was becoming an aftermath of the wreckage from the night before.

The people grew suspicious, distant and hardened. Resentment spiked conversations. Still, we walked the coastline, travelling further north, west and south, discovering 'Ireland' and, finally, rented a fine house overlooking the Atlantic. My last year was spent there mostly—the white surf from the sea staining the windows, the damp of that big bedroom with its awkward wardrobes and the endless talk tinged by anger, uncertainty and the curse of everything that looked like going wrong.

The previous summer had shown how fragile life actually was. Two of us were going to work June, July and August in the north-east of Scotland, building, of all things, an oil rig. We called down to Coleraine to book our flights and, wandering back to the little station, I could smell something acrid burning. In split seconds, a bomb exploded some way behind us. People came slowly walking towards us, bewildered looks on their faces, calling to other people in doorways and all the while streaming by us. They just kept coming and we called out to stay back, pointing at a solitary car in the road. But they kept coming and we turned into the railway station, stunned a little, disbelieving. In the train, there were just the two of us. You could hear a pin drop. When the second bomb went up, it felt like somebody had shouted out in the eerie silence of the carriage. We gaped at each other as the train pulled out. 'Jesus Christ,' Joe said, 'let's get the fuck out of here.' Within a year, we had all left that part of the country.

Of course, three years does not necessarily tell you much about a place. The triangle within which the university shelters retains its wonder because of all that happened there. But sifting through those years, I recall a craggy bit of the coast down below High Road when all you could see was the white spume of a turbulent sea and a rake of gulls, thrown up in the wind, screeching to their hearts' content. There was something exhilarating and disquieting about it—the dilapidated hotel with its broken windows and curtains flying out of them; all those tall houses closed in on themselves, as if the people were hiding. Maybe they were. Maybe we all were.

VII

Chalked up on the long and high blackboard was the legend: 'Give us ye John'. It was 1973 in what was called LT3 (or was it 1?) in 'phase one' of the recently, controversially built New University of Ulster. The university was situated in 1968 in the unionist stronghold of Coleraine rather than in the mostly Catholic city of Derry, where Magee College had been part of the Royal University of Ireland (1880-1909) and subsequently had prepared students for degrees from Trinity College Dublin.

A discordant building, it was nonetheless our gathering place with its wide open-plan lounge and 'refectory' where we watched television. Behind it stood the towers and concourse of the arts and science faculties and beyond them the magnificent river Bann cut a swathe through the farming land surrounding the market town of Coleraine and back out into the chill Atlantic. A landscape not for the weary or weak willed; 'bracing' is what it used to be called—brilliant at times and unpredictable, with the Scottish coastline in view on a good day.

The undergraduate students who assembled in that lecture hall thirty years ago were from various arts and parts of Ireland, Scotland and England. A couple of Americans as well. The experiment was straightforward—the last democratic flush of free education that had been extended throughout the 50s and 60s in Britain was now embracing, for various political reasons, the north-eastern tip in Northern Ireland. Build a university there and show that the political union with Britain is still alive and well and thriving. Befitting emblems of adversity. For outside the university all hell was breaking loose on the streets of Northern Ireland. Five years of political failure were turning into five years of bloody and vicious and intimate violence. The head count was very grim, very grim indeed. 1969: 19 deaths; 1970: 29 deaths; 1971: 180 deaths; 1972: 497 deaths; 1973: 263 deaths. Cruel crude figures never tell the story but spelling them out brings back the sheer horror of it all. A horror that we in our university refused to buckle under and the college life was vibrant, challenging, mind opening.

It's always unwise to think one can ever speak 'of' or 'for' a generation but certainly the cohort of students who passed through those early years of the new university in the 1970s experienced an intensity that is rare. Although, of course, we did not know it then, least of all as we sat there in LT 3 waiting for John Montague to arrive and 'give a reading'. We had actually arrived ahead of time and the graffiti writer (mind-blown like the rest of us, by *Moby Dick*, one of the term's key texts) and some other pals sat a few rows back waiting.

As it was known anecdotally at the time, NUU had turned into a working environment quite unlike (I imagine) what had been planned. The cultural mix of Protestants and Catholics from both sides of the Irish border, Scottish, English, some ex-colonial academics, some new left, some old left, some red-brick, some Oxbridge, some hippy, some unhappy, some visionaries of a kind, others soon to be disenchanted and yearning for 'the mainland' again. All added to the mix and created an atmosphere that had a truly democratic and liberal energy about it. The college acquiesced as Irish was promoted quite unselfconsciously as a language and culture available to all without political directives; the republican and unionist clubs cut up rough but no one was harmed in the thrust of argument—even at the most turbulent of times such as Bloody Sunday in January 1972 or after the IRA horror bombings of Bloody Friday in July of the same year. *1972.*

Writers visited the college quite frequently, if unobtrusively. J.G. Farrell, Louis Simpson, Tony Harrison and several Irish poets such as Thomas Kinsella, John Montague and Derek Mahon, who became the first writer in residence at the university. There was a very strong musical tradition being established in the environs of the college, as much as within, fostered by James Simmons, as well as by Liam O Dochartaigh, through the Irish language groups.

The Chieftains played some of their earliest gigs outside the Republic in the college. And here in 1973 we were waiting for John Montague.

Thinking back it's probably the case that he was promoting the newly-published *The Rough Field* (1972) or could it have been *Tides* (1971)? If his preface to the collection of his essays, *The Figure in the Cave* (1989) is anything to go by, he probably gave us all a bit of a lashing, one way or another. 'I find the element of self-seeking in the northern [Irish] thing depressingly close to *Ulsterkampf*, when our giant forbears, Yeats and Joyce, have given us the freedom of the world.'

While a little earlier in the same piece Montague remarks of Belfast, the city which a sizeable number of his audience that day would unquestionably have called home, that it is 'hard to think of Belfast as a parish, specially since no one has put it on the map. Belfast is of interest as a microcosm of the tensions that wrack the end of our century, the wall between the Shankill and Falls a miniature of the Berlin Wall.'

He was also none too impressed by the kind of support the North provided for him: 'hard as it may be to understand today [1989], there was no Northern dimension to Irish literature then, [the 60s], no question of going to Belfast for someone like myself, when even to get a little bourse to finish *The Rough Field* took nearly half a decade'.

Sentiments expressed more than fifteen years after that reading in LT1 but it wouldn't surprise me if Montague did indeed speak his mind that afternoon. Certainly I can remember his first remark, which was an immediate response to the slogan: 'Evangelical', he said, 'is that a biblical request! Give us ye?' Which went down very well with the troops in the front row, particularly the Scottish amongst us. (Those Glaswegian accents still carry in my head a kind of war cry. 'Give us ye!'). The subtexts of that room are impossible to relive now that so much separates us from that time. Maybe we didn't take ourselves too seriously, not really. Anyway the college bar called by early evening, and that was it.

VIII

In the springtime of 1973 the Belfast writer Brendan Hamill introduced me to Padraic Fiacc. Brendan was, like myself, a student at the fledgling University of Ulster, but he knew just about everyone who was writing in or about the north. Fiacc, he said, was thinking of doing an anthology on the north. I was writing and publishing poems here and there and so we should meet.

I hadn't actually met many poets up to that time. In fact, I don't think I knew any, so this meeting with Fiacc was important. He lived in the end house in a row of typical suburban houses in Glengormley, on the outskirts of Belfast. His home had been a stopover, at one time or another, for many of Ireland's best-known writers. Fiacc himself had been close to Padraic Colum. He was a very real link between the lost world of the Revival and the disintegrating world of Belfast. He also knew the work of Joyce (Fiacc's first book was called *By the Black Stream*, after Joyce's poem 'Tilly'), Beckett, most of the Classics, European writers like Mauriac, Baudelaire and there was that poem of Derek Mahon's, 'Glengormley' dedicated to Fiacc and published in Mahon's first collection, *Night-Crossing* (1968).

After our first meeting, I made a point whenever I was in town of seeing Joe (for he reverted to his real name when the defences went down and he became Joe O'Connor again). We would sit in the living room and talk about 'the situation' i.e. the Troubles, which was turning from bad to the worst it could be; and the domestic chores, which he religiously went through—lighting fires, clearing the garden of leaves, making coffee, spotting the return of birds, putting the 'garbage' out—an obsessed artistic temperament that was struggling with the break-up of his personal and social life.

What was going on in Belfast in 1973-74 makes for grim reading with nightly assassinations, bombings and this net of fear cast over the city. Every week, one or more would visit Joe; sometimes there would be gatherings. At one of these I met a young lad called Gerry McLoughlin, who wrote under the name of Gerry Locke.

He was like the rest of us. A Belfast lad who loved literature but couldn't sort out how it could relate to what was going on around him. When The Blackstaff Press published Joe's anthology, *The Wearing of the Black*, I was living in Galway. My girl and I travelled up on 14th December 1974 by train, Galway to Dublin, Dublin to Belfast. The party the next day was the last time we were to see Gerry McLoughlin. He was murdered four months later on 7th April 1975. His murder changed everything and it represents a terrible watershed in all our lives. I turned my back for several years on Belfast and the sickening reality of sectarianism.

IX

One Saturday night in the late summer of 1974 a squad of Welsh Guards threw a companion and myself against a doorway in the Clonard district of Belfast. This was 'an official army search' and, in assuming the necessary position, the two of us had to part some ways to let a resident in home, through his own door, between our spreadeagled arms. My companion, responding to repeated questions about who we were and what we were up to, blurted out that I did not belong to the area and was, in fact, a Protestant from the other side of town. He thought he was doing the right thing, of course, but the indifferent Welsh Guard perked up and replied, in fierce Cockney: 'A few of your lot copped it tonight, mate. Fancy a trip down the Village?' The Village was a fairly notorious loyalist enclave. He then lifted a paperback copy of Sheridan Le Fanu's *Uncle Silas*, a present I had been given earlier in the day, out of my pocket and, fumbling, dropped it into an oily pool of rainwater. When the Officer-Commanding stepped out of the armoured car, he told us to move on and ordered his men back inside. The book was destroyed so I left it there, swollen with rainwater, and walked towards another friend's house some way off, in the lamp-less dark, shadowed by the same soldiers in their Pig. I think that night I decided it was time for me to move on, to Galway as it turned out, in a matter of months.

I never really thought of myself as anything other than a Belfast man. When people talked to me and enquired about what it was like being 'a northerner', I really hadn't much of a clue. Because even though some of my ancestors came from County Fermanagh, my only real knowledge of the north was Belfast. I went to Sunday School and Church, joined the Scouts and lived a fairly typical boy's life growing up in the civil society of north Belfast: playing football, marking every season's changes with a different game, walking the streets, talking and smoking. I had no complaints. The world I knew was the world that I took for granted: 'This was the way it was' as Van Morrison says. Our district was predominantly Protestant: we had very good neighbours, some Catholic, some Jewish and other refugees who had married soldiers stationed in Europe during the war. There was a synagogue, grand Church of Ireland and Presbyterian churches, Baptist halls, evangelical Kingdom halls, one Catholic Church and so on.

My great-grandfather lived most of his life on the Duncairn Gardens. He was dead before I arrived but his influence was very strong through his daughter, Ethel, my grandmother with whom I lived. His name was Billy Chartres and he worked for the *Belfast Telegraph* and *Ireland's Saturday Night*. He was a staunch Unionist and a leading member of the Orange Order of his day and was an obsessive football man, having helped set up the Junior League. As a journalist he wrote under the name The Wanderer—which might have something to do deep down with his own family's spiritual roots as refugees at one time, or it may not.

Anyway, it took a long time to sort out what this invisible man meant to me. Although, as I say, I never met him, he lived in my mind and through photographs, press cuttings, cartoons and some family reminiscences, it took me ages to realise that William Bailey Chartres represented the past to me. He it was who dramatised the history of my immediate surroundings; his was the tradition that I could have

William Bailey Chartres (1868-1940), maternal great grandfather (photograph taken sometimes in the 1920s).

Mary Jane Quartz (1880-1949), maternal great grandmother.

Norman Maguire (1900-1961), maternal grandfather. Belfast born from Fermanagh family, married Ethel in 1926.

Ethel Rebecca Chartres (1900-1960), maternal grandmother, singer, in an early role sometime in the late 1910s, dressed for the part.

followed having thought about accepting a job as a 'cub' reporter at the *Telegraph* in the late 1960s. When I left Belfast he travelled with me, like a shade, and I had endless imaginary encounters with this Billy Chartres rebuking and chastising me, and ending up like Alfred Hitchcock walking through my poems when he got half a chance.

Often critics and journalists talk about 'Northern Protestants' as if they were dour, narrow, bigoted, unimaginative, mean, spiteful and so on. I am sure many are: as many as there are in any community in any place in the world. I get seriously fed-up though with the way journalists—with some honourable exceptions—and writers either pillory or patronise ordinary Protestants from Belfast as culture-less. I think of William Bailey Chartres and the family he came from and the one that came from him, which includes my friends, and me, and their families whom I knew growing up in the city. Whatever about their faults, or our faults, I do not see them the way they are portrayed so generally by the media. While it might involve a bit of hard work, like basic historical research, it doesn't take long to show the intellectual, cultural, musical, philosophical and artistic traditions that lie buried beneath the imprisoning stereotypical images with which northern Protestants are all too often treated.

Be that as it may, it took me a long time to understand that Billy Chartres was, in fact, my past and I had better try and understand it (and him) rather than run away. Indeed it took about seven years, from 1978 to 1985, living in Galway, starting a family, trying to find work, experiencing life there, travelling back and forth to Belfast, trying to explain what was going on—before Billy Chartres and I came to terms with each other. He challenged me and I responded as best

The Economics Boys: February 1967.
On a visit to the Prudential Insurance Co in Belfast.
Gerald Dawe, second along third row.

I could with a clutch of poems that eventually found their way into a collection of poems, *The Lundys Letter* (1985).

The Old Testament, the legacy of British military history, customs; the attitudes and experiences and desires of all the people I grew up with in the early 1950s and '60s, are at the core of what I wrote. Maybe the poems I am writing now are freer as a result, that is not for me to say.

My belief is that poets are poets first and citizens second. No matter what the religion, gender or race, poetry is the thing that matters. When people, be they politicians or professional commentators, proclaim that poets should write about this or that, that the poet must identify with this community or that—you had better watch out, because we are no longer talking about art but propaganda. Poetry, like music, or dance, or painting, or football for that matter, thrives when it is given its own space and hasn't some well-meaning, or not so well meaning, guru breathing down your neck. So my poems are addressed to whomsoever has the chance and cares to listen. I think of them in terms of Herman Melville's comment in *Moby Dick*: 'All these things are not without their meaning.'

I hate stereotypes. I hate the way Belfast is treated. I hate the one-upmanship and jockeying for position between different groups as if 'culture' could ever belong to one side to the disadvantage of the other. The basic truth about culture and art is that they cannot be segregated or worn like a badge of identity. It becomes something else then; a slogan, a form of superiority.

I hate all the tired, stale old arguments about this sense of identity being more natural, or historically valid than that—as if there were some Kryptonite which we have to possess to make us great or, at least, greater than the other. Writing poems, finding the language to do it best in, the forms and the voice, is difficult enough.

X

The thing that never failed to amaze me, however, about growing up in Belfast was that, once I moved outside it, no one had ever heard of my family. We were, how shall I say, unattached. We did not belong anywhere else in Ireland, even though parts of the maternal family could trace links with County Fermanagh. Yet, once out of Belfast, we were effectively in no-man's-land—whatever about further afield in London or, histrionically, in Huguenot France. I found this significant because the few writers I started to know something about—Irish writers, I mean—seemed to have connections all over the place. Not only did they know each other, but also they seemed to know every town and village throughout the country like the back of their hand. And someone always knew them, too.

In contrast we—my family—were, outside the city walls, anonymous. This was not a self-conscious policy, but it was an accepted, almost desired state of affairs. So in my head I compensated: Robert Lowell summered in Donaghadee, portly Wallace Stevens lived up Cave Hill Road; Elizabeth Bishop sat downstairs on the 64 bus, and Constantine Cavafy could be seen, on a very clear day, walking down Duncairn Gardens, minding his own business.

While in the real world, outside the library steps, or in front parlours, people confessed to writing poems. In school once, the headmaster commented on the fact that someone in assembly had a poem published and his name 'If I am not mistaken ... ' which I hotly denied. When I moved to the west of Ireland and non-stop reading, the names associated with Galway dropped like a mighty roll call: Yeats ... Joyce ... Synge. Breakneck stuff about The Tower and Yeats working away there. Or Joyce in Market Street, skipping along.

So it took the hundred miles and more between Belfast and Galway to get some balance right; to find a level, and to get things into perspective. This is probably why *The Lundys Letter* and the opening poems in *Sunday School* (1991) are set where I grew up, in north Belfast. It was not so much the place that mattered as the mood of a particular time there: the mid-1950s and early 1960s. The weight of that world fascinated me—post-war, Protestant—and the dominant view of the Cave Hill, always there, like the past itself, high above us. Whereas the lough lay seductively, promising adventure, and the hills beyond shone with sun and rain.

Sunday School was, in part, about that world, with its sense of scorn and disapproval; its inwardness and strength; its uncertainty and self-awareness; its survival; its distinctiveness. Bible stories, which had formed a kind of natural moral backdrop to our young lives, surfaced in several of the poems. Life had been 'proverbial'. We were told things through certain parables and I found this kept cropping up in the poems. Some of the poems in *The Lundys Letter* were similarly indebted to teachings from the Old Testament and, naturally, the images, which remained, of church going and school. But in leaving Belfast, like so many before me and since, I only found out what and where it was after that.

XI

The four lads at the back of the bus were talking. And then the rip of a metal tab as another can of Harp was opened.
  'The only fuckin' thing is Pernod and lime.'
  'Na. Harp and cider.'
  'He's a scar from thar to thar, the size of a fist.'
  My four and a half year-old daughter and I looked out the window. This was the last leg of a long, tedious bus journey from Galway to Belfast and the sun had come out splendidly. We were both tired and the conversation behind us grated on obsessively. They seemed so enclosed by their own world, violence at every turn of phrase, but when a Christian Endeavour student tried to engage them in talk, one of the lads offered her a swig of lager which she refused and fell silent. I thought she gave up very easily for an evangelist-in-the-making.

'Blowin' in the Wind', Easter 1970. Ballintoy, Co Antrim.

Every time I go home it feels that I inhabit two worlds, two timescales and that they are running parallel to one another. The walk from Glengall Street, now with my daughter and a few bags in hand, and the rush across Great Victoria Street, takes me by the site of Sammy Huston's Jazz Club: Frankie Connolly & the Styx, Sam Mahood & the Just Five, The Few, The Interns, The Method, and all those great bands that played there in the '60s and early '70s.

Thirty years ago: but I still find it difficult to write of that time or to reassemble in my mind my feelings and expectations, because as one of a group from widely differing backgrounds, the dangers did not seem so real. We grew away from Belfast, too, towards the allure of London and never thought that Belfast would succumb to the Troubles, like something out of Camus' *The Plague*.

We were, or some of us were, part of the Troubles, of course. It was important to understand what was going on—the marches, the political demands—but nothing, simply nothing, prepared us for the reaction either in terms of the mounting sectarianism—which we regularly had to circumvent—or the reality of the bombing.

When that came, effectively in 1970, our own lives took on a new weird meaning—we began to live more recklessly, with a perverse bravado, contemptuous of our backgrounds; we were like conspirators unconsciously losing contact with the usual ambitions and objectives of young men and women in their late teens and early twenties in an environment which was collapsing under its own weight. The contingency of living with and thinking about such hostilities encroached with ever-steadier tread in the mid-'70s, by which time a few of the group had been through university or art-school and most had left the north.

But the year that stands out in my mind is 1974. Returning to live in Belfast from university at Coleraine, I started to work as a librarian in the Central Library. I hadn't really given the future much thought, my own included, and work as a librarian seemed to be ideal. Maybe after experiences such as picking a child out of a bomb-blasted shop, having friends threatened and watching corners of the city steadily disintegrate into rubble, the time was impractical and inauspicious. Whichever way I look at it, I know that that year of 1974 was the eye of the storm. I can even point to a particular scene when all this became clear to me.

One lunchtime, going down through the cool airy stairway of the library, I recall becoming aware of a certain commotion at the swing doors, which opened out on to Royal Avenue. Making my way through a group gathered outside the library, between two bus stops and the red telephone kiosk, I eventually stood and listened to the clear intonations of a British army officer informing the large crowd on both sides of the street that a bomb had been located in a tailor's shop up the road from us. I knew the building well. It led round to Smithfield Market.

We stood, almost humbly, on our lunch hour, waiting, perhaps silenced, under instructions, irrespective of political leanings, religious inclinations, loyalties or whatever, depersonalised like a group of prisoners until finally the bomb exploded, a mass of shattering glass spilling on the ground, sundered brick sliding across the street to the squeals of women. Hesitantly at first, and then with more fluency, we went our separate ways. But just as the bomb went off, momentarily caught in the shockwaves that plumbed the street, I saw a careworn oldish woman, dressed in the usual sturdy, frayed overcoat and the workaday handbag, suddenly wince as if drowning in the sound of the explosion. Torn by its invisible pressure, she turned in a gasp into an image like that of Munch's 'The Scream'. I saw then how oppression works its way right through our very bodies and buries in our souls a physical terror that debilitates and makes acceptable the imposition of any final order. I think I also saw the deadly stasis of history captured in the English officer's poised language, in the blind gesture of violence and the ordinary drama of silently 'getting by' in our citizens' trail of survival.

It's really as if you had the choice of walking on two kinds of stairway—one fast, the other slower. Parallel stairways: this one is the present, the quick lane, of getting around the City Hall to a bus or taxi; the other, slowed to a measured pace, is the past. It's as if, thrown upon an imaginary screen, you can see yourself, going places, doing things, enlarged and selective. Nor is the experience necessarily unpleasant, but rather unsettling; 'a disconnect'. It makes your present actions and thoughts seem transparent, as you look through them to see the past and how much (or how little) has changed. It forces you to focus more often on what is really there, until you get into the way of this double take.

The taxi-man had a black plastic refuse bag in the back and said he was on his way to the dump when I hailed him. Where to? I told him and off we went, bouncing around, the faces of welcome at the familiar door as the taxi pulled up.

The week went quickly. I gave a few readings in schools; my own first, at Orangefield, in the staffroom this time, sipping coffee and working out old days and old 'pupils', walking along the same corridors and looking over the playing fields to the Braniel estate. I was still thinking, though, of the silent students I had just left, as they listened to this man talking about their school and the people he knew when he was there, about writing poetry and reading some:

> You staged the ultimate coup de grâce
> for the Union's son turned republican.
> I can see you shivering in the cold
> of an East Belfast morning, outside
> school, the bikes upended, the quad
> blown by a dusty wind, the rows of
> windows, some cellophaned, gaze
> back at the encroaching estate.

Next, over to Rupert Stanley College, sequestered in the East End, with the fabulous crane 'Goliath' like a vast arch of entry into the city. Then Sullivan Upper on the lough side, where an oil tanker edged out on the sea and a plane tipped up into the sky, leaving the coastline in slow motion:

> Deck chairs gape at the sun
> slinking down behind this part
> of the Irish Sea. Between us
> and the next landfall, trawlers
> criss-cross shipping lines
> fetching mackerel to Protestant
> villages along the shore.

On the bus back we had just a few on board, returning to Portadown, Armagh, or Monaghan, via a route of small villages all spruced-up and deserted on Sunday. The four young hard chaws weren't to be seen. I sat staring out the window and wondered which stairway they were on and how long they could stick it before they would feel that break in time, fastened for a second, as if the imaginary reel had broken down.

XII

So it took me almost seven years to unshackle myself from the confusions of the 70s, that had gathered throughout the early years of the Troubles into a very dark, and constrained first volume of poems, *Sheltering Places*. The seven years were all about relocating and seeing, quite literally, where and what I had come from—a typically Belfast Protestant hybrid of refugee and planter stock, with profound stability and instability masked under the surface of generations of adapting to and ordering northern society. When I wrote 'Secrets', sometime in or around 1980, it was as if a door opened and I could see something for the first time. I was commemorating a way of life: a codified landscape of home, family and the martial statues of an imperial past literally dotted around the streetscapes and imagined rooms of my childhood and youth.

Secrets

> I was coming-of-age in a sparse
> attic overlooking the sluggish tide.
>
> Down the last flight of stairs
> a grandfather clock struck
>
> its restless metronome to those
> who went about their business

Cover of Sheltering Places (1978).

with a minimum of fuss. My
puritan fathers, for instance,

stumbled from separate beds
and found their place

under the staunch gaze
of monumental heroes, frozen

stiff in the act of sacrifice;
they had always been

tight-lipped about God-
knows-what secrets.

About the same time I read A.T.Q. Stewart's *The Ulster Crisis: Resistance to Home Rule, 1912-1914*, a marvellous study written with a masterful narrative eye on iconography. Here's one of the leading Belfast businessmen of the time that Stewart quotes: 'You couldn't do better than take the old Scotch Covenant [1580]. It is a fine old document, full of grand phrases, and thoroughly characteristic of the Ulster tone of mind at this day.' Near-on half a million people signed the Ulster Covenant, including in Edinburgh, where it was signed on the Covenantors' Stone in the old Greyfriars Churchyard. It was the following passage that struck me like a thunderbolt when I read it first:

> The climax of Covenant Day came when Carson left the Ulster Club to go on board the Liverpool steamer. The docks were only a few minutes' walk away, but it took an hour for the wagonette, drawn not by horses but by men, to reach its destination. More than 70,000 people had managed to jam themselves into Castle Place, all of them intent upon getting

near enough to shake Carson's hand, and at the quayside they would not let him go. 'Don't leave us,' they shouted. 'You mustn't leave us.' When at last he got on board the steamer, aptly named the *Patriotic*, they called for yet another speech from him as he stood in the beam of a searchlight at the rail of the upper deck. He left them with the message they never tired of hearing, and promised to come back, if necessary to fight. Then as the steamer cast off he heard the vast crowd in the darkness begin to sing 'Rule Britannia' and 'Auld Lang Syne', and then 'God Save the King'; and as she moved into the channel rockets burst in red, white, and blue sparks above her, and bonfires sprang up on either shore of the Lough.

Within a year or so, I wrote 'A Question of Covenants', the title of which had come from an article published by the poet Aidan Mathews in the now-defunct literary journal, *The Crane Bag*.

A Question of Covenants
28 September 1912

> The *Patriotic* turns to face
> an invisible sea. From Castle Place
> thousands swarm through side streets
> and along the unprotected quays just
> to glimpse Carson, gaunt as usual
> who watches the surge of people
> call, 'Don't leave us. You mustn't leave us',
> and in the searchlight's beam,
> his figure arched across the upper deck,
> he shouts he will come back
> and, if necessary, fight this time.

It is what they came to hear
in the dark September night.
As the *Patriotic* sails out
Union colours burst in rockets
and bonfires scar the hills
he departs from, a stranger to both sides
of the lough's widening mouth
and the crowd's distant signing
'Auld Lang Syne' and 'God Save the King'.

The question I wanted the poem to dramatise concerns the contract and oath entered into in 1912 and how that view of history has been interpreted since in exclusively negative terms, as masking prejudice, bigotry, triumphalism, all of which is true but not quite the *complete* picture. Those hundreds of thousands of northern Protestants and unionists were also demonstrating (commemorating, if you prefer) a distinctive sense of identity. This is the Covenant they signed:

> 'Being convinced in our consciences that Home Rule would be disastrous to the material well-being of Ulster as well as the whole of Ireland, subversive of our civil and religious freedom, destructive of our citizenship, and perilous to the unity of the Empire, we, whose names are underwritten, men of Ulster, loyal subjects of His Gracious Majesty King George V, humbly relying on the God whom our fathers in days of stress and trial confidently trusted, do hereby pledge ourselves in solemn Covenant throughout this our time of threatened calamity to stand by one another in defending for ourselves and our children our cherished position of equal citizenship in the United Kingdom, and in using all means which may be found necessary to defeat the present conspiracy to set up a Home Rule Parliament in Ireland. And in the event of such a Parliament being forced upon us we

> further solemnly and mutually pledge ourselves to refuse to recognise its authority. In sure confidence that God will defend the right we hereto subscribe our names. And further, we individually declare that we have not already signed this Covenant. God save the King.'

In two years' time, in 1914, a similiar rhetoric would of course lead millions to their deaths. By the end of the twentieth century it would become utterly debased, an atrophied and hollow parody played out on the fields of Drumcree, the Catholic Church of Harryville, and on the streets of lower Ormeau. An afterglow of its honesty, however, still informs decent northern Protestantism—a scale of values suspicious of and often out of step with the media-dominated world of grievance-hood, cultural tagging and 'the narcissism of little differences'. A world view, which is, in fact, precisely that: a view of the world.

From writing these and other poems I saw part of my own cultural legacy as a northern Protestant, a more complex legacy, which had been repressed and pitilessly caricatured, demonised, and patronised as a cause of embarrassment in what were once called 'enlightened circles'. The unexposed relations between these various social factors represented an artistic 'poor showing'; Protestantism and the literary imagination parodied as an oxymoron, a contradiction in terms. So even though I stood (and still stand) in a severely critical relationship with that culture, and opposed to the inner history of its prejudices, I needed in some way to write it out of myself and identify its strengths: to commemorate.

If 'Secrets' is a poem about 'family', 'A Question of Covenants' is about 'community'. What links the two poems together are the patriarchal culture of northern authoritarianism and the imperatives of History: Edward Carson as leader as father figure, segued into my own great grandfather, that 'devout' unionist, William Bailey Chartres, of whom I've already written.

Of emigrant origin, with a relatively young and inexperienced, widowed mother and a younger brother to look after, living in Belfast in the late decades of the 19th and early decades of the 20th century, it couldn't have been easy. He worked hard and prospered, and his daughters—my Belfast grandmother and my London great aunt—seemed well set up for life. After writing a couple of poems about this man he disappeared. As one door closed, another opened.

Following the strange tales of family names like any genealogical root-searcher, I discovered that the woman this Huguenot William Bailey Chartres had married was called Mary Jane Quartz. Both had met in north Belfast, in a district of mixed religious and ethnic origins, the kind of district which seemingly did not exist in the north of Ireland, never mind Belfast. I daresay they buried their distinct histories in order to get on, a not uncommon strategy for emigrants, or children of emigrants. Mary's story, my great grandmother's story, needed its own form of commemoration. She became a subversive presence, a sociable, physical figure who handed on both the sociability and uncertainty of her own unconventional heritage, waddling down Royal Avenue in the middle of the road, stopping traffic, carrying a money belt under the ample skirts, yearning (one suspects) for a life beyond the seemingly leaden class conscious proprieties of her husband and the time. When I wrote the first poem to her, 'Middle

Names', another one came hot on its heels, called 'Quartz'. The poem tells a familiar emigrant story, apocryphal in part, about the journey of a generation of Europeans towards the end of the 19th century, duped by unscrupulous shipping companies or sea captains.

'Quartz' moves from the austerity and masculinity of the patriarchal order which had defined for almost two centuries the public face of Belfast, to *her Belfast*, and the vulnerable hope, in the midst of real personal challenge, of similarly courageous women making a life for themselves and their families, wherever and however they could.

Without laying too much freight on the slight shoulders of the poem, 'Quartz' meant for me an imaginative movement away from History to a personal voice, from power play to a yearning to live, imagining a different kind of cultural reality, by actually inhabiting none, albeit with that dash of the apocryphal. Maybe from these hidden, un-canonical sources a deeper sense of a common culture will surface in 21st century Northern Ireland, indeed throughout the country as a whole, and that these differences of background will be in future celebrated rather than locked away as idiosyncratic bit-parts in the big picture.

Quartz
for Katrina Goldstone

> So there is something I want to know
> great-grandmother, reclining on whichever
> foreign shore or ambrosial meadow,
> taking a second look at the old place—
>
> the valiant village, the provincial district,
> the back-breaking hill-climb to the apartment,

BIT PARTS

the quiet evening square in this country town
or that frontier post, down by the coastal resort

of some famous lake, say, with roman baths,
or a minority language—I want to know
who your grand dame was, or paterfamilias,
disembarking in a draughty shed, thinking

Liverpool or Belfast was really New York,
blinking in the greyish light of a noisy dawn,
looking out for a rooming house, or decent hotel,
putting one foot in front of the other,

taking the first right and walking, walking,
past the shipping offices and custom houses,
the rattling trams and carters and mill girls,
the steep factories and squat churches till the hills

converge upon this three-storied terrace
with the curtains drawn, the bell-pull shining,
and you pull the bell-pull and in whatever
English you'd learned you stepped in.

Selected Bibliography

Bardon, Jonathan, *Belfast: An Illustrated History* 1982
Boyd, John Archive, Linenhall Library Belfast
Bell, Sam Hanna, *The Hollow Ball* 1961
Bort, Eberhord, *Commemorating Ireland* 2004
Brown, Terence, 'Let's Go to Graceland' in *Studies on the Contemporary Irish Theatre* (eds. G.Genet and E. Hellengourach) 1991
Bruce, Steve, *God Save Ulster* 1986
Bruce, Steve, *The Edge of the Union* 1994
De Brun, Fionntan, *Belfast and the Irish Language* 2006
Buckland, Patrick, *A History of Northern Ireland* 1981
Carson, Ciaran, *The Irish for No* 1985
Charters, Anne, *The Penguin Book of the Beats* 1992
Clarkson, Leslie, 'The City and the Country' in *Belfast: The Making of the City 1800-1914* 1983
Collins, Brenda, 'The Edwardian City' in *Belfast: The Making of the City 1800-1914* 1983
Corcoran Mary P. & Peillon, Michael, *Uncertain Ireland* 2006
Craig, Patricia, *The Belfast Anthology* 1999
Edgar, David, 'The Victory of Inclusion', *Guardian*, 23 April 2002.
Fiacc, Padraic, *Odour of Blood* 1973
Foster, John Wilson, 'A Belfast Childhood', *Irish Literary Supplement* Autumn 1989
Foster, John Wilson, *The Titanic Complex* 1997
Grimble, Ian, *Scottish Clans and Tartans* 1973
Johnstone, Robert 'Stewart Parker: 1941-1988', *Honest Ulsterman*, No.86 Spring/Summer 1989
Kavanagh, Patrick, 'Poetry Since Yeats: An Exchange of Views', *Tri-Quarterly*, No.4, 1965

Kavanagh Patrick, *Selected Poems* (ed. Antoinette Quinn) 1996

Keats, John, *The Letters*, selected and edited by Stanley Gardiner 1965

Kerouac, Jack, *On the Road* 1958

Larkin, Philip, *All What Jazz* 1968

MacMathuna, Ciaran, *Traditional Music: Whose Music?* (ed. Peter MacNamee) 1991

MacNeice, Louis, *Collected Poems* 2007

Mahon, Derek *Antarctica* 1985

Maguire, W.A., *Belfast* 1993

Melly, George, *Revolt into Style* 1989

Montague, John, *Collected Poems* 1995

Montague, John *The Figure in the Cave* 1989

Parker, Stewart, *Three Plays for Ireland* 1989

Parker, Stewart, 'Me & Jim', *Irish University Review: James Joyce Special Issue* 12:1 1982

Parker, Stewart, *Dramatis Personae: John Malone Memorial Lecture* 1986

Power, Vincent, *Send 'Em Home Sweatin'* 1990

Sampson, David, *Brian Moore: The Chameleon Novelist* 1998

Sartre, Jean-Paul *Nausea* 1965

Stewart, A.T.Q. *The Ulster Crisis: Resistence to Home Rule 1912-1914* 1967

York, Richie, *Van Morrison: Into the Music* 1975